For T

‖

PAULETTE

with my best wishes

martin

PAULETTE

French by birth, English by chance

Martin Sorrell

First published 2018
by Impress Books Ltd

Innovation Centre, Rennes Drive,
University of Exeter Campus, Exeter EX4 4RN

British Library Cataloguing in Publication Data
A catalogue record for this book is available from the British Library

ISBN 13: 978–1–911293–16–3 (pbk)
ISBN 13: 978–1–911293–17–0 (ebk)

Typeset in Palatino
by Swales and Willis Ltd, Exeter, Devon

Printed and bound in England
by ImprintDigital.com

For Micou and Neil, *pardi*

Contents

Acknowledgements

To the following, for the help they may not always have known they were giving: Lorna Baker, Malcolm Baldwin and Anna Lunk, Sara Davies, Jane Desmarais, Margaret Duller, Hugo Frey, Trevor Hamilton, Andrew Joynes, Niall McCrae, Stephen Minta, Dave and Janet Mitchell, Katherine Slay, James Thomas, Andy Treacher, George Walker, Marilyn Wilson; to Susan Wicks for reflections on my first few pages, to Hilary Moore, Jen Russ, Frances Loeffler, Gareth Long and Harriet and Peter Poland for thoughts on an early chapter, and to Sandra Law and Chris Waters for responses to later ones; to Ruth and Trevor Preist for the use of their flat in Toulouse; to Richard Willis and Megan Symons at Impress Books for editorial guidance; to my sister and brother for memories all their own, and for checks and balances; and especially to my wife Claire, my good companion on all journeys for her forbearance, love and endurance – to all, my warmest thanks.

Who's Who

ix

THE ENGLISH AND HALF-ENGLISH

Keith (Sorrell) – Paulette's husband and author's father
Martin (Sorrell) – older son of Paulette and Keith; author
Micou (Marianne Sorrell) – daughter of Paulette and Keith
Neil (Sorrell) – younger son of Paulette and Keith
Daisy (Sorrell, née Peart) – Keith's mother
Frank (Sorrell) – Keith's father
Maureen (Heath, née Sorrell) – Keith's sister

Preface

The mid-1950s, a weekday morning, a quarter to nine; a house in Steyning, West Sussex. Five of us live here, three children and our parents. For all of us, a day at school lies ahead. The detritus of breakfast sits on the kitchen table, and it won't be cleared unless Paulette (our mother) sees to it, which of course she will. Keith (our father) has already left. He likes to prepare his classroom before his pupils arrive. Every morning shortly after eight, he walks along Station Road, passes St Andrew's Church, skirts Chantry Green, and ten minutes later arrives at the Grammar School. I (eldest child) am about to head there myself, but on my own. It would be a serious loss of face for a boy to be seen arriving with a parent, particularly when that parent is also a teacher there. Micou (sister, younger) and Neil (brother, younger still) have already walked the three hundred yards to their little school.

Only Paulette remains. Her school is in Hove, and the train she really mustn't miss stands in the station below, ready to leave. Mr Tombs, the porter who happens to be our next-door neighbour and knows our habits, stands sentinel on the station forecourt, looking up at our house, waiting for Paulette. He can't hold the train much longer; the timetable is the timetable. But Paulette is clearing dishes into the sink and food into the larder. Only when everything's tidy does she grab her bag of books, lock the front door and run down the steps to the station. As she goes, she signals to Mr Tombs, who a minute ago had to send the train on its way. He sees Paulette, darts back inside, climbs the footbridge and waves his red flag at the train, now a hundred yards clear of the station. The driver spots the flag, and ignoring rules and regulations, slams into reverse and brings his train back to the platform. Mr Tombs opens the nearest carriage door and ushers his neighbour aboard:

"Another flying start, Paulette."

Taunton, Somerset, 11th May 2010. I'm remembering that battle and so many others my mother had with the clock. I'm outside Waterstones waiting for an old friend. He and I are going to have lunch together; it's many years since we've had the chance. We made our arrangement yesterday at Paulette's funeral. The time is 12:45 and already he's quarter of an hour late. At 1 pm there's still no sign of him. I try to tell myself it's not his fault. He has an awkward drive from where he's staying, thirty miles away. But suddenly I snap. I'm full of a rage that has caught me by surprise. I turn on my heels and stomp straight back to the station. A train down to Exeter is there. I jump in and an hour later I'm home. I make a pot of tea and take it upstairs, where I run a bath, as hot as I can bear. When the foam is starting to spill over the edge I lower myself in.

In the evening, I phone my sister, then my brother. We go over yesterday, the funeral. We review, compare, digress, choke a little and try to laugh. By the time we're through, it's almost midnight, too late for the tea that nevertheless I make and stand drinking at a window. I'm watching the lights of the city below, all of them white except the one red eye of a crane-mast. I'm musing on Paulette, not her battles with the clock, but a different struggle. She wanted to write her memoirs, but it never happened. Whenever she tried to wield Time's pencil, she stalled. On a good day, she'd manage a few lines, no more. But the day she chanced on Lorna Baker's little recording company, she found her true medium, and over several afternoons, she spoke effortlessly into a microphone, unscripted and unrehearsed. She sparkled, she laughed, she charmed. The six CDs that resulted were her way of telling the story of her life and the people and places in it. This book is mine.

1

Braseros and *Bourriols*

The box of family mementos lies open in front of me. It's a mock-Treasure-Island chest, kitsch, studded with brass and fastened by straps and buckles. In it are the cuttings, certificates, scrolls, letters and photo albums that are the record of five generations of the family to which I belong, French on my mother's side, English on my father's. I'm searching through the French part. Before me, slightly torn, is a school photo, taken not long after the turn of the twentieth century. I locate the two relatives Paulette's note has named on the reverse. Third from left, next to last row, my great-aunt Jeanne, aged seven or eight. She looks as though she's just poked her tongue into a bad tooth. Behind her is her older sister, my grandmother, known always as Mitoune. Both girls wear their hair looser than the others, but apart from that there's not a great resemblance between the two of them. Jeanne's face is mobile and energetic, Mitoune's regular and still. I can see the beginnings of the beauty that would strike people so much.

We often heard about two of these people in particular. One was a painter: Gorm Hansen, a Dane who on his way south to the sun stopped off in Auvergne and never left. He'd been captivated by the mountain landscape and the inhabitants. At some point, he met the Tourdes family, and was fascinated by Mitoune. On canvas after canvas, he tried to capture her beauty, and time after time he failed, though one of the failures,

1

Portrait de Mme A.T., made it to the 1928 *Salon des Artistes Français* in Paris. It's ghastly, in large part because Gorm has given Mitoune a footballer's five-o'clock shadow.

The other man who fell under her spell was no less a figure than Paul Doumer, the radical-socialist parliamentarian who was to become President of France in 1931 (only briefly; a year later, he'd be assassinated by a Russian émigré). I don't know how serious Doumer was about Mitoune. He was devoted to his family, but in 1920, when he first met Mitoune, he must have been in emotional turmoil as no fewer than five of his eight children had been killed in the war just ended.

The school in the photo is an *école communale*, a primary school. It appears to be single-sex. There's not a boy anywhere, unless I'm being fooled by unisex smocks and hair styles. I'd hoped also to find the two girls' elder brother, Jacques. Perhaps he was now at a *lycée* somewhere else, or perhaps he'd already been taken out of school and sent into the fields to mind the cows. Because I know there was a period in his adolescence when he had to do the *transhumance*, the transfer of cattle from high to low pastures, or low to high, according to the season. It was hard work, often in harsh conditions. He'd be out all day driving the animals, and at night he'd find shelter in a *buron*, a hut where he bedded down on a platform immediately above the cattle so as to catch the warmth of their breath. It did poor Jacques no good. He'd have weak lungs for the rest of his life.

I work out that the school photo must have been taken in 1907, when Mitoune was not quite twelve years old. A mere seven years later, she was married; less than two years after that she was pregnant with my mother, Paulette.

*

We have a running joke in the family that whenever Paulette was asked a straightforward question on a straightforward subject, her answer would always begin at the beginning:

Q: "What made you leave Auvergne?"
A: "Well, you see, I was born in 1916."
Q: "How did you meet your husband?"
A: "Well, you see, I was born in 1916."
Q: "Why did you go into teaching?"
A: "Well, you see, I was born in 1916."

As indeed she was. On 20th July to be exact, in the village of Jussac, a little north of Aurillac, the capital of Cantal, the most south-westerly *département* of Auvergne. Auvergne, note. Not *the* Auvergne.

"It's not THE Auvergne, *titi*, not ever. You don't say THE Somerset, THE Exmoor, do you? It's the same. Auvergne."

Family members, regardless of age and gender, were always *titi*, pronounced *tee-tee*. The noun is Victor Hugo's. *Titi parisien* is what he calls the street-urchin Gavroche in *Les Misérables*. Paulette's grandchildren repaid the compliment by calling her *tita*. Sweet and exclusively feminine, I thought, until I learnt that the large gondolier who was Lord Byron's manservant went by the same name.

So, in late July 1916, Paulette Marie Eugénie Jacqueline was helped into the world by the local *sage-femme*, midwife to Jussac and surrounding areas, and quite possibly deliverer of lambs and calves as well. Paulette used to claim that as she'd been listening in the womb to the bagpipes and accordions playing downstairs, her feet were dancing the *bourrée* as she emerged. Musicians – farm-workers, road-menders, the odd pen-pusher from the town-hall down the road – would often gather in the house where she'd be born. They came to play whenever there was something to celebrate, a birthday, the harvest, a *Fête*. The biggest *Fête* was *La Sainte-Marie*, Jussac's patronal day, 15th August. Paulette's earliest reliable memory was of the *Sainte-Marie* in 1919, when she was three. She remembered the intoxicating sound of the *cabrettes*, the Auvergnat pipes that are played by squeezing its bag under one elbow. She remembered being led onto the dance floor by a tall man. It

3

wasn't him, though, but the accordion player she fell in love with, on account of his fast fingers and his brilliantined quiff. He was from Paris, and for that reason went by the city's nickname, Paname. She also remembered – although this was perhaps a memory from later years – the plum tarts baked for the occasion by her grandmother. Sounds and tastes that were so strong in Paulette's memory, she promised if she smelled plums or heard the *cabrette* at her funeral, she'd jump out of her coffin and join in the fun.

Paulette and Lili, aged 7 and 3.

Paulette's mother wasn't christened Mitoune, but Jeanne Antoinette. The nickname Mitoune may have been adopted to avoid confusion with her sister, also Jeanne, though I suspect that it was part of a longer name which I've never come across. French first names work differently from English; they're sometimes hyphenated, making them double- or triple-barrelled. How *Mitoune* came about, I don't know. Certainly, it's an endearment; the *-oune* ending says so. Normally it would be just *-ou*. For example, the man Mitoune would marry was called Pierre, but was always known to us as Pitou. That happens to be First World War slang for a private soldier, which is exactly what he was for a few years. My sister's name Marianne soon morphed into Micou. That could be a variation on *michou*, in Auvergne a word for a small loaf of bread. My brother Neil was transformed into Iannou, from his middle name, Iannick. The *-ou* ending is like the *y* that gets added to English names: James to Jimmy, John to Johnny, dad to daddy.

The house where Mitoune gave birth to Paulette, and where Mitoune's brother Jacques and sister Jeanne also lived, was rented by their mother. She, Eugénie Combier, known to all as Grand'mère, was a strong-featured, strong-willed woman, brusque and loud. Paulette adored her. She's there on a few photos in our treasure chest. I must say she looks formidable in the English sense (not French *formidable*). It's partly the stern look on her broad face, and partly the hairstyle, between a loaf and a cushion. She was no beauty. In fact, the more I see images of her, of her family, indeed of any Auvergnat, the more I marvel at Mitoune. She was definitely the one who got away. Auvergnat women don't become pin-ups or film stars, except Audrey Tautou. The men even less so. Their short legs and big noses aren't suited to the cinema, unless someone were making a film about Vercingetorix and his peasant army who gave Caesar's legionaries a bloody nose at Merdogne. (Don't look for Merdogne on the map. You won't find it. The name

5

was so unfortunate that Napoleon III decreed it be changed. *Merde*-ogne has become Gergovie. No more schoolboy jokes about the Battle of Shit Creek.)

Mitoune was just twenty when Paulette was born. Four years later, in Aurillac, she was to have her only other child, Marie Louise Françoise. She was known to most of us as Lili, but to some others as Zerline, though what her association with the wily lass in Mozart's *Don Giovanni* was, I haven't the faintest idea. Lili was pronounced *Lee-Lee*, sharp and French, not the soft English "lily". As Mitoune never took well to motherhood, it was fortunate that Grand'mère was there. In fact, Paulette said that it was she who was her true mother. Mitoune couldn't handle the rough and tumble of infants. Perhaps it was her temperament, perhaps she'd come at it too young. Marriage had come fast on the heels of her first encounter with Pierre. The pair first set eyes on each other when some errand brought him to Grand'mère's house, and apparently it was the *coup de foudre* on both sides. He was five years older than she. It's obvious why he should fall for her, but she for him? Pitou wasn't handsome or dashing. In the photos taken at the time, there's something about his eyes that hints at the mental instability that would affect his life and that of others. Already he seems a diminished man.

At five feet two inches, Mitoune looks tall. It's her bearing. Even in old age there'd be something regal about her, though in fact she came from the humblest stock, generations of peasants who toiled on the land. Her family name was Combier, common in Auvergne, and more pleasant on the ear than the married name she acquired, Tourdes. Pitou held that name in high regard. He thought it was a corruption of La Tour d'Auvergne, and that he belonged to a forgotten branch of the nobility. In truth, the name was as lowly as his wife's. It derives from Latin *turdus*, thrush. My grandfather Pierre Tourdes was more Peter Thrush, bird-catcher, than Sire Pèire of the Tower of Auvergne.

In the summer of 1914, only months after Mitoune and Pitou were married, the First World War broke out. Pitou had to rejoin his regiment immediately, leaving Mitoune in Aurillac. Apart from infrequent periods of leave, that was the last he would see of Auvergne for five years. On the day Paulette was born, he was somewhere in eastern France with his unit, which we'd always believed was a regiment of cavalry. However, when I did some research, I came across a document issued after the war by the Committee of the Légion d'Honneur, detailing the award of its Military Medal to Pierre François Tourdes, *canonnier* in the 210th Artillery Regiment. *Canonnier*: Pitou had been a gunner, an artilleryman. We'd known for a long time that by 1916 he was at Verdun and involved in France's longest and costliest battle, as great a trauma to the French as the Somme was to the British. Now that I knew his real regiment – or thought I did – I found out which operations the 210th undertook. These were the facts: in late February or early March, it was deployed to the Bois d'Avaucourt as part of a wider plan to take back the area from the Germans. The assault was launched on 29th March, and fierce fighting continued through the day. By nightfall, the 210th had made significant gains. Much of Avaucourt wood, though not all, was in its hands. But a large proportion of the regiment was killed, including its commander Lieutenant-Colonel de Malleray, and an even greater number wounded, so many casualties that the survivors were first withdrawn and then relieved by the 227th Regiment of Infantry. The remnants of the 210th retired to the Bois de Fays, and in due course were redeployed elsewhere under a new commander.

So it seemed Pitou had been a foot soldier at Verdun, not the cavalryman of family myth. Nor had the injuries which left him semi-lame been sustained on horseback. No longer could we believe the story that he'd been on a reconnoitring mission when he was shot by a German sniper, and that with awful precision the bullet contrived to pass straight through one foot, the horse's belly, then the other foot. Nor that the horse dropped dead, and from somewhere a comrade appeared and hauled Pitou to safety. I no longer knew quite what to believe, but as I was about to put the final full-stop to this memoir, Micou rang me to say she'd found some papers in a wrongly-labelled folder. In a battered logbook I found the facts of Pitou's war. Finally the truth emerged.

Pitou enlisted on 2nd August 1914 and served for the first eighteen months of the war in the 16th Artillery Regiment and not in the 210th as I thought I'd established. He fought in a number of battles, but in 1915 was sent away with dry pleurisy and exhaustion, presumably to a military hospital. In February 1916 he was transferred to the 36th Regiment, and it was with

Pitou. Verdun. 1916.

that regiment that he served at Verdun and took part in the battles of Bois de la Caillette, Bois de Vaux-Chapître, Fleury and Woëvre. There's no mention of any injury. It was not until April 1917 that he was transferred to the 210th, a reserve regiment. Why he ended up with them, I don't know. My guess is that the hell of Verdun had rendered him mentally unfit for combat. Certainly he was physically able, because it was a full year later, on 1st April 1918, that he received his crippling injuries. The 210th was in north-eastern France near the river Oise, as back-up to the 10th Regiment. On that day, Pitou had been put in charge of a convoy taking supplies to the Front. The logbook doesn't say whether the convoy was motorised or horse-drawn, but I suspect the former. A shell exploded as they were passing through the village of Dompierre, and Pitou is variously recorded as receiving shrapnel wounds to his right foot and left thigh, or both legs but not his feet. In a second logbook, I read that he ended up in Bordeaux, in a military hospital on boulevard Nicolas, and that from 9th August to an unspecified date his injuries were treated with both physio- and radio-therapy. As there's no more information and because this was virtually the end of the war, I'm assuming that Pitou was kept in hospital until the Armistice and then demobbed. Or he may have stayed in hospital as he doesn't reappear in Aurillac for at least another year. As his mental state may have been worse that his physical injuries, I wonder if he wasn't sent to a French equivalent of Craiglockhart. There was a hospital of that type in Limoges, not too far from Auvergne.

Pitou had gone off to war severely emotionally damaged by a shock he'd received at the age of ten. On the occasion of his First Communion, the young man whom he'd always understood to be his older brother revealed that he wasn't that at all, but his *father*. Henceforth, Pitou should address him as *papa*, not Albert. And the woman Pitou had thought was his mother in fact was his *grand*mother. That, according to Paulette, was a deception that suited her perfectly as she'd made no bones about wanting more sons. Paulette re-created the scenario. *"Ce petit sera mien,"* that lad will be *mine*. The secret that had been kept dark was that the eighteen-year-old Albert had had a brief liaison with an older woman and she'd become pregnant. Not much is known about her, except that she was roughly ten years older than Albert, and went by what I've always assumed was a nickname: Coco. Either affectionate – Little Coco – or snide – Coco La Cocotte. But it turns out it was her surname, spelt Cauquot. We have one photo of her,

Albert, left, and Pitou. Circa 1914.

a studio portrait. Her face, not conventionally beautiful, is interesting and attractive. She looks very alive. I've searched for a family resemblance, but haven't found it. She gave birth to Pitou in February 1890, and soon after, she was gone from Aurillac. Two explanations have circulated of why she left in such a hurry. Pitou's was that to avoid scandal the Tourdes packed *La Cauquot* off to Saint-Malo, and left her there to pine alone. The version we heard from Paulette was quite different: *Mademoiselle* was a flighty number who wanted nothing further to do with her son.

Mlle Cauquot, Pitou's mother. Date unknown.

"She was after the fast life, *titi*."

"What, in Saint-Malo?"

*

As was common in so many families during the war, there were relatively few men around, young ones anyway, in Paulette's very earliest years. Mitoune's brother Jacques was in the Navy, serving on a destroyer in the Dardanelles. Joseph Nozières, the man Paulette's aunt Jeanne would later marry, was away on a battlefront somewhere in the east of France. Grand'mère's husband, who should have been present, given that he was past fighting age, had long since vanished. He'd walked out on his family and gone to live with his sister on her farm. Although that farm was only a few villages away, Paulette would never meet him. She didn't even realise he still existed. Nobody seemed to know why he'd cleared out. Paulette's hunch was that he couldn't cope with Grand'mère, who was, as the French say, *tout un personnage*, quite a character, strong and forceful. She needed to be. There she was in Jussac, uneducated and without marketable skills, the lone breadwinner with several mouths to feed. The vanished husband sent her no money, and the State *allocation familiale* (family allowance) was yet to be introduced. All Grand'mère had to fall back on were her wits. Paulette remembered two of her commercial ventures, though there may have been more. The first one was a barber-cum-hairdresser's salon. Grand'mère wasn't trained, but that wouldn't have mattered. To judge from photographs of women of the time, most Auvergnates had the same cushion-loaf hairdo as Grand'mère herself. As for men, one big pair of scissors and a cut-throat razor were enough.

But the hairdressing salon failed to make enough money. So Grand'mère opened a cafe instead. The front room was ideal. As her home had formerly been the Hôtel Chandon, aperitifs and coffee might once have been served there. It was a spacious and sunny room in a house generously-proportioned. At one end there was a barn, home to ducks, chickens, tools and bric-a-brac. At the other, a room let out to an old peasant woman of very slender means, known as Ata. (I've no idea if that was short for something, Atalie perhaps, or a nickname, or her surname.) Behind the room which became the cafe was another smaller one, which the family preferred to use, more

From left to right: Jeanne, Grand'mère, Mitoune, Ata. Outside Grand'mère's house, Jussac. Circa 1910.

intimate, and the easiest to heat. It was dominated by a huge hearth in which people could place their chairs for maximum warmth. There was space for four, one of which was known as the *chaise à sel*, the salt chair, because of its extra function of keeping salt dry in an attached box.

From the adjoining kitchen came aromas of whatever was cooking. Stews and casseroles in copper cauldrons or trays of meat roasting; at breakfast, the buckwheat pancakes, *bourriols*, that were Paulette's favourite. In the evening, there might be a *ratatouille*. Or a *soupichette*, the diminutive name given to a vat of vegetable soup, bulked up with chunks of bread and enlivened by dollops of red wine. In winter, there was sure to be *truffade*, a crusty bake of sliced potatoes, goose fat, and quantities of Cantal cheese, the classic dish of Auvergne. And once a year, in February, there'd be a bonus when Ata returned from a week on a farm over towards Mauriac, where she'd been to help butcher the farmer's best pigs. She'd arrive back bearing packets of bacon and sausages for everyone to share, and for several days after she'd join Grand'mère in her kitchen to prepare a celebratory feast.

For those who didn't get a place in the hearth, there were other ways to keep warm, or try to. One was the *chauffrette*, a square box inside which was placed a copper pan of hot embers. It was closed by a lid dotted with holes to let out the heat. You had to stick your feet on it in such a way that it didn't burn you. It worked beautifully for the lower leg, Paulette said, but the rest of you went on shivering. I can well imagine. I'm looking at a *chauffrette* now as I write, one of the items that was shipped from Auvergne to us in England in the 1980s. It makes a nice ornament, but it's easy to see how ineffective it must have been.

Another source of warmth was a more substantial contraption known as a *brasero*, a copper container which like the *chauffrette* would be filled with hot embers. It would be placed under the table at meal-times or when people gathered socially, say for a game of cards. The trick was to use a long and heavy tablecloth which would hold in the heat. But in effect the *brasero* was only a *chauffrette*, if a bit larger. Your legs got the heat but your back still froze. What's more, untended *baseros* sometimes caused fires, mostly small though occasionally a house did go up in flames. And they'd been known to asphyxiate people asleep in unventilated bedrooms.

Mains electricity and water didn't reach Jussac until the 1930s, well after Paulette had left. In her day, it was all paraffin lamps. That's what the womenfolk worked by, sewing and darning into the evening, and ruining their eyesight. Water had to be fetched first thing every morning from the well in the backyard, in mid-winter no one's favourite chore. Until it was done there'd be no coffee and no breakfast to get the day under way. Paulette remembered, or perhaps misremembered, that it was always she who drew the short straw. She'd grumble about it every day – except Monday, laundry day.

"I loved it," she told us. "I didn't have to be asked twice to help."

She could recall the procedure in detail. Two large trestle tables would be set up in front of the house and cauldrons of boiling water brought out. Grand'mère and her lodger Ata would spend the whole morning pummelling sheets, pillowcases, table-cloths, towels, clothes. When that was done, a wheelbarrow would go back and forth, taking load after load down to the river to be rinsed. Then came the wringing-out – by hand, of course. Finally, the barrow would be reloaded, and the whole lot would be wheeled to a nearby hedgerow and spread out to dry. The next day or the day after, depending, came *le repassage*, the ironing. Two flat irons heated on the stove, one for Grand'mère, the other for Ata. Paulette sat with them and learnt.

Even better were the errands Paulette ran to the shops up by the church in the centre of the village. She'd be sent to fetch meat from the butcher, bread from the baker, thread from her favourite, the haberdashery, whose owner always gave her a boiled sweet or a stick of liquorice.

Towards the end of her life I asked Paulette what summed up those first years of her life.

"Oh, laughter, freedom, air. And love, most of all."

2

War Damage

Pitou came back to Auvergne on leave occasionally, but it wasn't until well after the war was over, in 1920, that he returned to Aurillac for good. (It must have been in the first months of the year, given that by April Mitoune was pregnant again.) All but one of the menfolk connected with Paulette made it back from the war. Mitoune's brother Jacques survived the Dardanelles; Joseph Nozières, the young man from Marmanhac who would shortly marry Mitoune's sister Jeanne, got back from the trenches completely unscathed. The only death I know of was one of the Tourdes extended family. I know of him only because his name appears on the war memorial in Aurillac's main square.

Pitou's wounds had healed well enough to let him shuffle around. But he'd become uncontrollable. He lived permanently on the edge of violence, and carried a loaded pistol everywhere he went. People thought him deranged, but in reality he was suffering from shellshock. Damaged in mind as much as body, Pitou was a *mutilé de guerre* on two counts.

For his pains, he received a handful of medals. Before we contrived to lose them, I made a list:

Croix de Guerre, 1914–1917, avec palme
Croix du Combattant
Valeur et Discipline. République française

Médaille Philippe Pétain, Maréchal de France. Chef de l'Etat Médaille de Verdun. 21 février 1916. "On ne passe pas"

The sixth medal had no inscription. It was a red metal star set against a laurel wreath and hung on a ribbon bearing two much smaller metal stars.

Most of these medals were recognition of service generally, and endurance. But the *Médaille de Verdun*, inscribed with the celebrated motto *On ne passe pas* (They shall not pass), must have been awarded for the series of offensives he took part in there.

I still have four items which connect me directly to Pitou. One is his Omega pocket watch, slim, silver, elegant and which I can't think went to war with him. It sits on my desk, unwound and in need of overhaul. The second is a large sheet of poor-quality paper that's been folded in four. It's *La Ligature*, no. 18, 10th June 1917, *Journal Humoristique Satirique Et Insecticide*, a French equivalent of *The Wipers Times*, four pages of gallows humour. The many little anecdotes, the wonderfully-drawn cartoons, are very moving and oddly heroic. They give a good sense of ordinary men trying their best to preserve their sanity. The third and fourth items, both postcards, are the most personal as they contain the only examples I have of Pitou's handwriting. One has a semi-saucy image of a little girl with the face of a doll. The French caption says the card is censored; the English one tells the censor not to look. Neither the name of the addressee nor the date appear anywhere. Pitou is in a state of agitation. His unit is near Soissons, north-east of Paris, in the killing-fields, after a rest period in Paris, where nobody paid them much attention or even seemed to know a war was being fought in their name. The other card is dated and addressed. It was sent to Mitoune from Neumoulins on 14th September 1915, a few months before the Verdun debacle and around the time Pitou went into hospital with pleurisy. The picture on the obverse is inscribed *La Grande Guerre 1914–15*,

Chauconin près de Meaux. Six medical orderlies stand around a staff car in the hamlet of Chauconin, forty kilometres northeast of Paris. The scene is tranquil; there's hardly anything military about it. The medics are described as both French

Card from Pitou to person unknown. Written near Soissons. Most likely 1918.

and German. Were they neutrals, early doctors without frontiers? The reverse of this card, like the other, is crammed with Pitou's tiny handwriting, every available millimetre. He's left no space for Mitoune's address, so I assume it arrived in an envelope. Or maybe it was never sent. As it's full of detailed information, I wonder if the censor blocked it. I'm struck by the way Pitou addresses his young bride as *Très chère amie*. No English translation quite gets the sense, formal yet tender, polite but intimate. Pitou seems conscious of his style, rather literary, and which in the last sentence trips over itself. Here's the whole message as I've translated it:

> *Très chère amie,* We're making the journey from Choisy to Villers-Cotterets in stages. We'll pitch camp in the forest between Villers and the Front. It's the end point of Saturday's final stage – 90 kilometres in five days – which have been hard because of the weight we have to carry. Since we left Neumoulins we've been crossing a part of the country which is going to become very familiar to us. Ruins, roads lined with graves. We stopped at a memorial this morning to pay our respects to the men who fell at the Battle of the Ourcq, the prelude to the Battle of the Marne. It was on these plains that the encounter which forced Von Kluck to retreat took place. Now's not the time for day-dreams about the banks of the Seine and the Marne. No more boating on the river, no more sorties to Paris. No sooner do I begin my life as a soldier than the moment arrives when we'll be asked to do our duty as Frenchmen. Morale is good, health excellent, and I'm not lacking in courage. Only the absence of *ma petite amie* is hard to bear. I protect her memory jealously and always conjure up her image during periods of idleness and boredom. She's the ray that lights the dawn of homecoming and towards which all my thoughts aspire to see.

*

Pitou's father Albert did his best to set his son up professionally. His first plan was to give him a position in the Tourdes business, long-established and well-respected. It specialised in the restoration and renovation of important public buildings, churches and châteaux. Albert's plan should have worked. Pitou was skilful with his hands and could have made a very competent draughtsman. But his indiscipline scuppered everything. Albert's next plan was to set Pitou up in a shop the company owned in Aurillac on the present rue du Rieu. Pitou would run it, and his family would live above the premises. Business cards were issued; we have a stash of them in our treasure-chest. Customers, we learn, will find all the "oilcloth, linoleums, wall paper, mirrors, windscreens, window glass, stained glass, prints, engravings, objets d'art, artists' supplies" they might need. In addition, "stone-cutting, bevelling, polishing, silvering, and picture-framing" can be undertaken in the workshop. Above the shop there were three floors for the family. On the lowest of these were the kitchen and the dining-cum-sitting room. On the middle floor, two bedrooms, and on the third, two further rooms, rarely used. On the ground floor, behind the shop itself was another kitchen. And underneath the lot was the cellar, not for wine, only junk and cheeses. Apart from the pristine business cards, the one souvenir we still have of that shop is the marble statuette of Dante which accompanied Paulette all her life, and now sits in Micou's house.

The role of shop-manager didn't suit Pitou. He became, if anything, an even greater liability than before. He'd lurk about the premises, and if, for example, someone brought in a painting to be framed and it wasn't to his taste, he'd refuse to do the work. Instead, he'd insult the owner. Before long, Mitoune had to take charge, initially to Albert's great displeasure. The Tourdes hadn't welcomed her. They'd been opposed to the marriage from the outset. The Tourdes didn't marry peasantry. It took time for attitudes to soften. Eventually, Mitoune's calm and dignity won Albert round. He became reconciled to her running the shop, which she did to the best of her ability while her husband frittered the day away. He'd developed something of a routine. He'd spend an hour or two in the atelier that Albert had provided him elsewhere in Aurillac, then would put down his brushes, take to the streets and fetch up in some bar or cafe. There, he'd order a glass of wine and start talking about the war to anyone who'd listen. He had story upon story to tell, of trenches, mud, shells, comrades who'd died, comrades who'd survived. The more he talked, the less sense he seemed to make. People took him for a drunkard, and so did the family. The truth was, however, that he hardly even touched his wine.

Pitou, Mitoune, Paulette. March 1918.

How did Paulette fare in such dysfunction? Not well. For one thing, she hated Aurillac. Although only a few kilometres from Jussac, it was a different world. She'd had to exchange the freedom of the countryside for the oppression of gloomy streets, the open-heartedness of Grand'mère and Tante Jeanne and Ata for the stiff manners of the Tourdes. She soon fell ill. Realising why, the doctor prescribed the one medicine that would work: she should go back to Jussac. She did, and for the next three years she lived a life split between Aurillac and Jussac. Between 1920 and 1923, she journeyed back and forth on the bus, unaccompanied, but in the care of the driver whom everyone knew and trusted. Paulette's divided life might have gone on longer had not Grand'mère's circumstances forced a major readjustment. Like the hairdressing salon, her cafe had become unviable. Besides, she wanted to be with her daughter Jeanne, who now had two small children and was living a good few kilometres north of Jussac. Jeanne's husband Joseph had found employment on a remote farm there.

From now on, Paulette must live full-time in Aurillac, and start formal education. At the age of seven, it was high time. But for a while she refused to go to school, and neither of her parents did a thing about it.

"I'd been left to grow up like a weed, and that's how it could go on as far as they were concerned."

Albert took charge, and got his granddaughter a place in Sainte-Geneviève convent school. And he paid the fees. For all his stiffness and reserve – Paulette sometimes spoke of the excruciating lunches to which she was summoned by Albert's maid, and which passed off in total silence – Albert was an honourable and generous man, and a loving grandfather. It's no wonder that Paulette would say that the two adults who'd done most to bring her up were not her parents but one grandmother and one grandfather.

Her education got off to bad start. Physically, she'd be at her desk, but in her imagination she was back in Jussac. She'd be there skipping across fields, wandering the woods and hills, sitting in her tree-house. Every afternoon, she'd will Albert's maid to arrive and take her away. Which sometimes did happen, though usually Paulette had to join the crocodile that was marched by two *religieuses* to the collection point on the square.

Paulette's first year of schooling went badly; the second went worse. She wouldn't work, she wouldn't co-operate, she offered only passive resistance. She'd find herself banished to the corridor, where she had to stand still for hours, her nose touching the wall. She fell hopelessly behind. By the age of nine, she still could barely read. At home no one helped; the indiscipline continued. If, as often happened, Paulette said she didn't want to go to school that day, Mitoune simply said "*Alors, n'y va pas.*" Don't go then.

But around the age of ten, matters improved dramatically when Paulette was assigned to a new teacher, one who was interested in her, could see her potential and stopped letting her get away with things. Paulette changed overnight. Her reading caught up and soon she overtook the rest of her class. She conformed and cooperated; she paid full attention to everything her teacher put before her. So, a few years later, she easily obtained the *Certificat d'Etudes* that allowed her entry into the *classe du Baccalauréat*. In British terms, she sailed through her GCSEs and began on A-Levels. Which is when it all started to go wrong again. She was given another teacher, so incompetent, so frightening that she failed her next set of exams. As they were in her strongest subjects, she had to switch to maths and science, her weakest.

Bad luck attracts more bad luck. Paulette had started to learn the violin, and was doing well under a teacher she liked. Then she lost that teacher as well. The replacement was a semiblind woman who, unable to use sheet music, played and taught by guesswork. Every finger position she made Paulette adopt was wrong. Albert arranged for Paulette to be sent to a competent teacher, but the damage was done, and she abandoned the violin for good. She was beginning to drift as she had at the age of eight and nine, but then she was introduced, presumably by a new teacher, to Spanish. It was a revelation. She hadn't got on well with the dead language of Latin, but here was a foreign language that was immediate and *alive*, and was speaking to her. She knuckled down and made such rapid strides that she began to think she might go to university.

Meanwhile, things were not improving at home. Pitou's mental state had worsened, and he'd abdicated any responsibility that he still had. An exasperated Albert had decided to disown him, at least informally since it wasn't possible to do so in law. Pitou was ranting more furiously, raving more wildly than ever, until one day something in his brain gave and he collapsed in the street. He was rushed to hospital, and there he remained for over a fortnight while doctors tried this and that to sort him out. They were successful to a degree, because he was returned to his family in a surprisingly tranquil state. It was in this period of peace, Paulette remembered, that he had the good sense to keep out of everyone's way and do the one thing he truly enjoyed and which soothed him: fly fishing. Most days he'd take himself off in the train to one of his two favourite rivers, the Truyère and the Cère. He'd ask his daughters to accompany him, and occasionally Paulette accepted. (Lili would have none of it, neither fishing nor her father.) Those expeditions brought Paulette the closest to a happy relationship with her father. She'd sit on the river bank and watch him working rod and net with skill and grace. He'd be content to stand for what seemed like hours in the middle of the stream, silent and still. It was during those hours, Paulette always thought, that he came the closest to conquering his demons. Hours which brought out the tenderness in him. As they sat eating their picnic, he'd explain the art of fly fishing, the sort of bait to use, how to hook it to a line, then how to cast the line. He evoked the beauty of the trout, for

25

him the supreme fish, king of the river, and the adversary he respected most.

There was one day in particular Paulette like to recall. Pitou and she were standing together midstream in the Cère. Pitou had cast his line a few minutes earlier when he tapped Paulette lightly on the arm, put a finger to his lips to shush her, and pointed. A kingfisher was coming upstream towards them. It passed in a flash of blue and vanished, but a moment later reappeared, flying towards them, and alighted on the high point of Pitou's arching rod. There it perched, its body riding the movement of the rod, its head perfectly still as it fixed its eyes on the water. Eventually, seeing nothing worth the dive, it took off again, switching on its coloured lights.

Pitou's state of calm was only temporary. Soon he was going downhill again. Mitoune was less and less able to cope, either with him or the shop, which was in serious trouble. A few months before Albert washed his hands of his son, he'd spent close to fifty thousand francs of his own money to bail the shop out. Now he was refusing to step in again. In desperation, Mitoune turned to Paulette and begged her to put all thoughts of university aside. She, Paulette, was their only hope. She must find a way of earning money. Couldn't she offer private tuition around the town? Didn't that pay well? Surely there were wealthy families with youngsters about to sit French and Spanish and Latin exams?

The more her family declined, the greater became Paulette's sense of responsibility. She decided therefore that she had no choice but to do as Mitoune wanted. She put advertisements around the town, and got takers. What she earned must have made all the difference. The shop wasn't closed; the family wasn't ejected from rue du Rieu. Life could stumble on.

*

Summer 1935. It's not clear to me how, but the financial crisis had receded. Paulette had just turned nineteen and had left school armed with her *Certificat d'Etudes*. She was free to plan her future, and she decided it had to be outside Auvergne. She was thinking in terms of Spain. It so happened that among her private students there'd been some nuns from Barcelona, temporarily in Aurillac as volunteers for a charity. When they returned to Barcelona, they invited Paulette to stay in their convent. The invitation came at the perfect time. Paulette had been bitten by the Spanish bug. Everything: the literature, the landscape, the music and dances, but most of all the language. So she said yes to the nuns, and one winter night under a sky full of stars brighter than anything she'd imagined, crossed the Pyrenees.

She didn't stay very long with the nuns. Catalonia wasn't where she wanted to be, not because of the political situation – if she was aware of the rumblings that would explode into civil war, she wasn't disturbed by them – but because she wanted to better her knowledge of Castilian Spanish, not learn Catalan. The obvious place to be was in a language school in Madrid, and so she presented herself one freezing morning in the first week of 1936 at Barcelona railway station with the exact money for a one-way third-class ticket to Madrid and a taxi at the other end. The booking-clerk told her she must travel in first class, however.

"I couldn't understand the reason, but there was no argument. The only extra money I had was for the taxi. Fortunately there was a nice man behind me in the queue who offered to pay the difference. I accepted, which I suppose was naïve of me. But he was the perfect gentleman. He didn't want anything in return. He found me a seat and then took himself off to another carriage."

Once she arrived in Madrid, Paulette decided to get a taxi anyway and borrow the fare from her landlady. But, to her dismay, the landlady hadn't yet got back from the Lycée

27

Français, where she taught. So Paulette asked the cab driver to take her there, only to find that the landlady had just left. Their paths had crossed. The day's second Samaritan materialised, this time the Lycée's caretaker, who paid the taxi and sent it and Paulette to its intended destination. When finally they met, the landlady was taken aback by her young French guest. Paulette Tourdes didn't seem the *jeune fille raisonnable* she'd been led to expect. She must be a flighty creature, got up in Parisian clothes and taking taxis everywhere. Nor did her opinion of Paulette improve in the following days and weeks. *La señorita francesa* spent too little time at her studies and too many hours in cafes in the company of unsavoury characters.

"I may have looked sophisticated, and tried to act the part, but I was anything but a flirt, I don't think I led men on. But they did seem to hover around me. I only wanted to talk about things I found interesting, art, literature, politics."

Talking politics in cafes was getting risky. The Second Republic, Left and liberal in complexion, and barely five years old, was fragile and under assault from the Right. It had already seen off one coup attempt, and feared more. During February, Paulette's second month in Madrid, the ultra-right-wing rebel General Franco had been relieved of his command and despatched hundreds of kilometres away to the Canary Islands, where he set about organising an invasion of the mainland and the overthrow of the government. By July, the country was in crisis. Military uprisings, orchestrated by Franco, occurred all over Spain. In response, the government armed civilians to combat the mutinies. The atmosphere was febrile. Street demonstrations erupted everywhere, pro- and anti-government alike.

Paulette continued to go about her business, to and from her classes, in and out of cafes and friends' apartments. She managed to keep out of trouble until the evening she was caught in a particularly violent demonstration. Rocks and stones flew, windows were smashed, and blood flowed. Paulette dived under a table and stayed there until enough calm was restored for her to risk the streets. She rushed back to her lodgings, only to find that the church in the next street had been set on fire. From the safety of her room, she watched as people fled, among them priests whose cassocks spread like wings as they ran for their lives.

One night, the *sereno*, the night-watchman who patrolled Paulette's district every evening, wasn't there. *Serenos* were an age-old Spanish institution. With their great bunch of keys, they let people into their apartment blocks. They also kept an eye on things, like the plain-clothes policemen which to all intents and purposes they were, the authorities' eyes and ears. Paulette's *sereno* was something of an exception, a gentle old soul who took a shine to her, and always let her in without too many questions when she came home at an unreasonable hour. The next night, he wasn't there either, nor the next, nor any after. It was only days later that Paulette discovered that her friendly watchman was an ardent communist who'd been "disappeared".

Then, in the middle of July, came the siege by Franco's rebels of the Montaña Barracks, on the western edge of Madrid. The soldiers inside remained loyal to the government. Aided by workers' militias, it took them two days to beat off the assault. A great number of lives were lost on both sides. The Spanish civil war had begun in earnest.

It was time for Paulette to leave Spain, not at all what she'd planned. She'd hoped to stay on indefinitely as a teacher of French. Instead, around the time of her twentieth birthday, she took the train to France, only to discover that the political situation was as volatile, if not as deadly, as the one she was leaving. The two-month-old *Front Populaire*, the coalition government led by the socialist Léon Blum, was already in trouble, and at least for a while civil war in France was not an impossibility. Jewish Blum himself was always in serious personal danger, and in fact a few months before, members of a royalist and anti-Semitic organisation called *Camelots du roi* – street-hawkers of the king, nothing to do with King Arthur – had dragged him from his car and clubbed him savagely.

Paulette arrived back home in Aurillac to find that there as well the situation was dire. Pitou again was being impossible, if anything more than ever. But worse, headstrong fifteen-year-old Lili had decided to play up, and was getting beyond Mitoune's control. And the shop was under such threat that Mitoune turned once more to Paulette. And once more Paulette fell into line, resumed her private lessons, and through the autumn of 1936 and into 1937, kept the shop afloat and the family together.

It's at this point that Paulette's recollections became confused. She could say only that the next months were "a tricky period". With the help of what's in our treasure chest, I've pieced the story together. At some point Mitoune hatched a plan to decamp to Le Havre and join her brother and sister and their families. Big seaports such as Le Havre held far better prospects for Jacques and Jeanne than did Auvergne. With luck, it would be the same for Mitoune. Her idea was to take only Lili with her and leave Paulette behind to look after Pitou and run the shop, the penalty for being so efficient. She, Mitoune, would do what her own mother, Grand'-mère, had done in Jussac. She'd run a cafe or perhaps a guest-house. As Jacques was now doing well as a businessman, he could underwrite her. And of course she'd be near her sister.

So long as Paulette continued to bring in money, Mitoune's plan remained a contingency. But then, whether by agreement or not I don't know, Paulette downed tools and left Aurillac, this time not for Spain but to the University of Toulouse, where she enrolled on the Spanish course. In the event, she didn't stay long. Perhaps because he thought her exceptionally talented, her tutor said she should transfer to Bordeaux University to study under the country's leading authority on Spain. There was a second reason why Paulette followed his advice: nagging family duty. Not wishing to implement her Le Havre plan yet, Mitoune wanted Paulette home again, and Bordeaux University

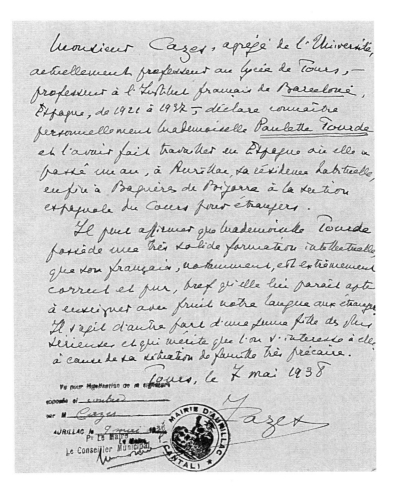

Character reference for Paulette from a teacher. 1938.

would allow Paulette to be a distance student, based in Aurillac. For a third time, therefore, Paulette found herself advertising private lessons in the town and handing the proceeds to Mitoune. Twice a term, on the rubber-tyred trains known as *Michelines*, she travelled to Bordeaux. There, she met her tutors and attended the lectures of the famous professor. She lodged with the aunt of a school-friend in a street called, ominously in view of what was coming, rue du Tondu, Shaved-Head Street.

It was at about this time that Paulette was drawn into her first romantic relationship, or at least the first she was prepared to reveal. A young Romanian doctor was on secondment in France to gain more experience, and had been sent to the hospital in Aurillac. Whether he'd been involved in Pitou's care during his two weeks there and had run into Paulette then, I don't know. It took him little time to declare his love for Paulette and his desire to marry her. His name was Gerstein or Gerstentein, Paulette couldn't remember which, nor his first name. She did recall that people warned her that he was after only one thing – a passport. For a Central European Jew in the 1930s, a French passport was worth a marriage. But – Paulette couldn't or wouldn't recall – the romance foundered. I suspect she realised she was being taken for a fool. She put the doctor out of mind, and re-focused on her studies, an exciting part of which would be an international summer school in the Pyrenees, designed to bring together young Europeans in the spirit of friendship, shared knowledge and peace. The venue was a town with the slightly comical name of Bagnères-de-Bigorre, situated almost within shouting-distance of a country setting the worst example. The Spanish civil war was raging, and when the wind blew from the south, you could hear the boom of the guns.

At the close of the summer school, Paulette returned to Aurillac. Mitoune's shop managed to limp through the winter of 1937–38, but by the spring it seemed finally that the game was up. But then in May, when Mitoune was days away from throwing in the towel, Albert died, and that rescued the situation. Though the bulk of his estate went to his wife, Agnès Delom, whom he'd married in 1924, under French law a proportion had to pass to his son. In a twist of irony, feckless Pitou saved the shop, the family and the roof over their heads.

Paulette went on to complete her studies at Bordeaux University, and obtained a degree. Equipped for a career – which

Paulette. Circa 1937.

she'd decided would be teaching – she prepared to make the break with Aurillac. She might well teach abroad. This time it wouldn't be to Spain, for a couple of good reasons. One: the civil war was still in full cry. Two: at the summer school she'd met an intriguing young man from England, and that's where her thoughts were turning.

3

Hardy Country

When Keith Sorrell and Paulette met and shook hands across the refectory table at the summer school, it may have been something of a *coup de foudre* for him. For her it was more a *coup d'indifférence*.

Keith was finishing his undergraduate studies at London University, where he read French language and literature. He attended Queen Mary College, in the East End, but was living with his parents in Southall. Every day therefore he'd cross London twice. In the spring of 1937, on a short break in Brittany, he entered an essay competition advertised in a national newspaper, and came second. I'm surprised he didn't come first; his essay would have been the model of how to do them: thesis, antithesis, synthesis. His French style would have been classical and pure, down to the subjunctive of the obscurest verb. His prize was a fortnight at the Bagnères-de-Bigorre Summer School, all expenses paid. There, he enrolled on the French course and, as Paulette had opted for the Spanish, their paths crossed only at mealtimes. But after a few days, when their group at table decided on a mountain hike, they were thrown together properly.

The idea was that the group would climb the Pic du Midi, all 2877 metres of it, and stay in a hostel overnight. From the outset, the climb was tricky and demanding. Paulette, used to mountains, had no problems, but Keith soon was having difficulty breathing. The asthma he'd had since childhood still affected him, especially if the air was cold.

"I took hold of his hand and gave him sugar lumps which I soaked in lemon juice," Paulette said. "He made it to the top, and once he'd got his breath back, he and I stood there for a while in silence, it was so beautiful. That's when we *really* met."

In the hostel, the whole party, male and female, stayed in one room, on the floor inside sleeping-bags. Paulette found herself between Keith and someone called Aidan. All through the night, Aidan tried to take hold of Paulette's hand. Keith watched, said nothing but seethed with fury. In the morning, the party made the descent to Bagnères. Keith again had to fight for breath. Paulette stayed with him, and they fell behind the rest. Once back indoors, Keith was given a room on his own so that he could be monitored. Ignoring the rules, Paulette took him soup and stayed with him unchaperoned until she was ordered out. Once Keith was on his feet again, they spent

Paulette, right, and friend. Bagnères-de-Bigorre. 1937.

more time together. He'd never met a young woman so excitingly un-English; she'd not come across a man so inward, un-French and austere.

"He wouldn't come skiing or dancing with the rest of us," Paulette remembered. "Not because he didn't want to, but for self-discipline. He told me one day that if he wanted an apple, he'd put it on the sideboard and stare at it, willing himself not

Keith and Paulette. April 1938.

to pick it up and eat it. I was intrigued. He was such a contrast to my father, the only man I knew, really."

Back in their own homes after the summer school, Keith and Paulette started a correspondence. All their letters would have been in French as Paulette knew very little English. Two months later, Keith's parents issued Paulette an invitation to spend Christmas with them in Southall. Keith had had to work hard on them. They didn't much care for what they'd been hearing about this young foreign woman. Keith wrote to prepare her for a few shocks: his family, English food, Southall, the weather. So Paulette turned up in ski boots, quilted jacket, padded trousers, hat and gloves. Keith was at Victoria Station to meet her. They took a bus to Paddington, then sat among commuters on the train to Southall, shocked that everyone seemed so tired. Keith's parents, Frank and Daisy, welcomed Paulette with courtesy and few words. They were, Keith had warned her, quiet people.

"I could see where Keith got it from."

Frank was the local station-master who'd risen steadily through the ranks of the Great Western Railway. His manner was rather stiff. Daisy was more relaxed, and over the next days, the atmosphere improved. Paulette's cheerful attempts to speak English went down well. Her accent was an extra charm. For her part, Paulette saw that Frank and Daisy were decent people, straightforward and good-hearted. At the end of her stay, Paulette went back to Aurillac on warm terms. The visit had been a success, and even though war was looming, she began to apply to schools in England for a post as *assistante de français*. She wrote the drafts and posted them to Keith, who checked them and returned the corrected versions, which she copied out and sent off to each school. Keith urged her to go for what he considered the nicest parts of the country, the counties along the south coast.

"He especially loved Dorset. He was always telling me about Thomas Hardy. Years later, when my English was good enough, I did read his favourite novel, *Jude The Obscure*. I've never felt so depressed in all my life."

Dorset is exactly where Paulette was offered a post, and in September 1938, around the time of the Munich Agreement, she arrived at South Lytchett Manor, a girls' boarding school housed in a stately home midway between Hardy's Havenpool (Poole) and Anglebury (Wareham), and where she was thrown among staff who loved to hate anything and everything French. And not only the staff. The girls were just as bad.

Fortunately, Paulette was assigned lodgings in the cottage of two very likeable people, Mr Toop, the school gardener, and his wife.

"We got on like a house on fire. Mr Toop was small and bouncy, like a sprite with mad hair and thick moustache. He laughed all the time and told funny stories. Mrs Toop was quieter. She was taller than him, and had a podgy face. It was a relief to be in their company after class, I can tell you. At weekends, they'd take me to Poole and Bournemouth on the bus, and on the way back, we'd stop off in a pub with the strangest name, St Peter's Finger."

Paulette's handicap at that school wasn't just that she was French. She wasn't a patch on her predecessor either, as she was reminded every day. But with the help of the Toops, she toughed it out for the full school year. At the end of her contract, she visited Keith in Southall, then returned to Aurillac.

*

Keith's attachment to Dorset had been formed early, during summer holidays on a farm in Corscombe, a village set deep in Hardy Country and an hour's drive west from Lytchett Manor. For much of his childhood, Keith and his parents and his sister Maureen spent every August there. The tenants of Court Farm were two of Frank's and Daisy's oldest friends, Tom Durden and his wife Gertie. For Keith those summers were the same idyll that Jussac was for Paulette. They were for Maureen and their parents too. So much so that Frank and Daisy requested to be buried in Corscombe churchyard. I know Keith would have chosen the same for himself, but it wasn't possible. Instead, we put a bench in his memory next to his parents' grave.

June 2016, a Saturday. My wife Claire and I are in Corscombe to look for Court Farm. It has been many years since we were here last, and we're not sure we'll find it. We arrive where we think the farm ought to be. A traffic marshal in a high-visibility jacket is blocking the road. Are we here for the Corscombe Fest, he asks. The car park is that field over there. No, we answer, we're looking for Court Farm. Are we close? No idea, he replies. He's not local, he's from Beaminster. And then he lists all the good things we'll find if we go to the Fest. It's only £2 per head. Why not, we decide. We have time. We'll look for Court Farm later. We pay, park the car and stroll over to the large quadrangle formed on three sides by farm buildings, on the fourth by a lovely old manor house. Claire's beginning to think we've been here before. Maybe when we explored Corscombe on the day Keith's churchyard bench was inaugurated. There's something very familiar about that tithe barn, she says. We make our way there. A sign at the entrance advertises Pets' Corner, 50p per person. Claire pays and goes in. A couple of minutes later, she's out again to report two puppies, four kittens and a stroppy pony. The lady on the door asks if we'd like to take away a pair of those lovely kittens. A plastic money bucket sits between her feet and in her hand there's an empty glass. Sorry, we say, we can't manage even one. Never mind, says the lady, and introduces herself. She's Venetia, and we are? We tell her our names and Claire asks her if this happens to be Court Farm. It is indeed, says Venetia, and she and her husband own it. Hence she's sitting there, hence the money bucket. I ask her if the name Durden means anything.

Oh, the Durdens, she says. We know them terribly well. One of them helps us on the farm a few days a week. They're sure to be here this afternoon.

A family with little children arrives to see the animals in the barn, so we slip away and park ourselves on the grass to listen to a bagpiper in a long blue mediaeval dress and a white bonnet. She's playing a merry ditty, and she's very good indeed. No wonder. The old gentleman we're next to on the grass tells us that she's principal bassoonist in the London Philharmonic Orchestra. The ditty comes to an end, and after the applause, the piper announces that what we've been listening to is an ancient Dutch air which hasn't been heard for centuries as she herself discovered it only recently in a library archive. For her next number, she produces a small wooden puppet and manipulates it with one hand while she plays her pipe with the other. The puppet jolts its arms and legs in perfect synchronicity with the music. It's a tour de force. This, our piper reveals, was inspired by an illustration in the Heidelberg Book, and is entitled *The Dance of The Dead*, a tale of the Grim Reaper, terrified villagers and an ancient mystic merrily leading everyone off to the afterlife.

We leave the music and stroll out to the moat beyond the buildings. A tall, angular man sits in a plastic chair that's way too small for him. He's deep in conversation with someone, but gives us a wave and gestures us to take a seat. Is it that he thinks he knows us? Neither Claire nor I have seen him before, but we sit. We look around. The moat looks neglected, the water not visible below a carpet of duckweed. On the other hand, the grass around the moat has been freshly cut, and is luminous in the sun that bursts through for a moment, catching as well the weathered tiles on the barn's steep roof.

Then the tall man is ready for us. He wants to talk to us because he's our host this afternoon. He's the owner of Court Farm, Venetia's husband, John, and he wants to talk with as many guests as possible. So, are we enjoying ourselves?

John must be in his late seventies, maybe older. His pullover is more holes than wool, his trousers not much better. Farm muck has discoloured his trainers. The way his hair is, it might have been combed with a stick. His razor has mown his cheeks well enough, but his neck is a ruff of snow-white down. He's a man perfectly at ease with himself, relaxed and charming. He wears his ruff with distinction.

He tells us about Court Farm. It has quite a history. It's in the Domesday Book and it was once attached to Sherborne Abbey. It even played a minor role in the birth of the United States; a set of texts on political revolution somehow found their way from here to Harvard University a few years before the Declaration of Independence.

John interrupts himself as someone he knows well is passing, and he wants to tease him with a jibe about the imminent EU referendum. As neither man is wearing any Leave or Remain badges, my assumption has to be that landowner John, no doubt public school and probably Oxbridge, is a Brexiteer, and his friend a Remainer. It turns out to be the reverse, as I discover when the two men throw friendly insults at each other. John has been a fervent internationalist all his life, he tells us. He's dismayed – no, hopping mad – not only that the referendum has been called in the first place, but that it's been boiled down deliberately to just two issues, both misrepresented. He's written several letters about it to *The Times*; the latest should be in Monday's edition.

He asks us the time. (His watch doesn't work.) We tell him, and he excuses himself. He has to circulate among his guests. He bids us good afternoon, and as he unfolds himself from his chair, warns us of the ghost of Court Farm. A ghost in broad daylight? Oh yes, says John, the White Monk will appear at any time. He always wears a white habit and a cowl, which is why no one has ever seen his face. John himself thought he saw him one day. A figure was standing among the trees, white from head to toe. As well as the cowl, it even wore a mask. But when it spoke, John heard Venetia's voice. Dressed in a bee-keeper's suit, she was off to collect honey.

Back in the main area, we listen for a few minutes to the band that's replaced the piper. Twenty ukuleles and a washboard are putting on the agony, putting on the style. Venetia spots us and beckons us over. The Durdens have arrived. Do we want to be introduced? Or can we find them ourselves? It's easy. One is wearing a lime-green jacket, you can't possibly mistake her ... And indeed we don't. She's part of a group of four coming away from the dog show behind the manor house. We introduce ourselves and learn that they are grandchildren of Tom and Gertie. We chat for a minute or two, and then Linda and Annette say that they're going up to the churchyard at four o'clock to put fresh flowers on their family grave, so why don't we all regroup by Keith's bench?

By 4 pm, Claire and I have made our way along the path beside the church and the newer graves, then past the older headstones, badly weathered, half-collapsed. At the top end by the perimeter fence, we've reached Keith's bench. It's wearing well even though over the years it's changed colour. Lichen has turned it a greyish-green. Some of the lettering on Keith's parents' grave has faded and become illegible. Keith had wanted the site refurbished. In fact, he and I made a start two years before he died. But we didn't get far, and since then nothing has happened. Today, all I do is take a few photos. When the Durden group arrives, more photos are taken, and then we're given a tour of the churchyard. From one angle, we see just how big the church is, disproportionate given the size of the population it has to draw on. Linda tells us it's where the Durdens have always been baptised, married and buried. They still are, and she hopes they always will be.

For the second time today the sun breaks through. This time it stays out and everything around takes colour. To the east, the green of the fields lightens the higher they reach. To the west, we have to shade our eyes to make out the trees on the hilltop. This is Dorset at its best, as Keith would have wished to remember it. When our family came to choose an inscription for his memorial bench, we decided on four simple words from a poem by Paul Valéry about another graveyard: *Ce lieu me plaît*. This place pleases me.

4

Land of Hope

On her arrival home from Lytchett Manor in July 1939, Paulette found that this time, finally, after so many cries of wolf, no if or buts, the shop was doomed. Whatever funds Pitou had inherited from his father, they were gone. Mitoune had put into action her plan to relocate to the Channel coast, but now without the need to split the family in two. No one would be left behind. A family guest-house had been found, a *pension de famille*. Mitoune and Lili would manage it jointly.The location was Trouville, a beach resort almost as fashionable as its next-door neighbour Deauville, and favoured by painters such as Monet and writers such as Flaubert and Proust. It was only a boat ride across the mouth of the Seine to Le Havre and Mitoune's brother Jacques and sister Jeanne and their families. Jacques was establishing himself in the shipping business, and Jeanne and her family were there because the port and the town's heavy industries offered her husband Joseph better prospects than farming in Auvergne.

In the one photo I've found of the *Hôtel Pension Florida*, Mitoune and a pretty young woman in a flouncy white dress are framed in an upstairs window. The pretty woman is Manette, Jeanne's daughter, Mitoune's niece. A sign on the façade advertises *Confort Moderne* and *Cuisine Bourgeoise*. The two women look happy, and in fact that summer in Trouville

45

From left to right: Jeanne, Jacques, Mitoune. Circa 1914.

lifted everyone's spirits. Keith came to stay, and the whole of Paulette's family warmed to him. His Englishness was thought charming, especially by Mitoune. Keith was her idea of the English gentleman, distinguished in his tweed suit, courteous, reserved, but friendly and unstuffy too. (And, Paulette began to think, Mitoune was the mother *he* should have had.) There was a sense, in the holiday atmosphere of Trouville, that the luck of the Tourdes at last had turned. They might even think of staying on permanently at the *Forida*, especially if Jeanne and Jacques planned to remain.

It wasn't to be. Towards the end of summer, the war that had been threatening became imminent. Keith had to hurry back to England, and the Tourdes decided they should get back to Auvergne. Paulette went with them. It's not clear what happened next or even where the family lived, assuming the apartment over the shop in rue du Rieu was no longer available. But it's a reasonable bet that Paulette's private lessons came to the rescue in the months that followed, that quiet period of the Phoney War known in French as the *drôle de guerre*, the strange or the funny war. However, undaunted by her experience at Lytchett Manor and eager to return to England and teaching, Paulette made several applications and in due course was offered a temporary position as *assistante de français* in Bradford Girls' Grammar School for the summer term of 1940.

"I thought it was safe to accept. In France we kept hearing that if it did turn into full-scale war, the Allies would wrap things up in no time. They'd camp on the Maginot Line and keep the German army stuck behind theirs, the Siegfried Line. Germany would starve, and Hitler would surrender."

In Southall, Keith was expecting his call-up papers any day. As a conscientious objector, he knew what he must do: refuse to attend the initial medical. When he was summoned again, he'd refuse again. He'd then be ordered to attend a Tribunal, a hearing before a magistrate and a couple of respected members of the local community. By and large, Tribunals were not well disposed to conscientious objectors, and proceedings were perfunctory. Keith knew what to expect. He'd be offered alternatives to bearing arms: service in an ambulance unit or fire-fighting or agricultural work. Keith intended to refuse them all and accept the consequences, which almost certainly would mean imprisonment.

Before Paulette accepted the Bradford post, Keith wanted to make it clear to her that neither he nor England were good prospects. Paulette wavered, and for the only time she could remember, Mitoune intervened with firm advice: ignore Keith and go. And so she did. In April 1940, she took the train up to Paris, crossed to Gare Saint-Lazare. The Dieppe boat-train was packed with military personnel. She managed to struggle aboard a carriage full of Polish officers and heavy with tobacco smoke. She put her head round a compartment door and all the men leapt to their feet. They insisted Paulette have a seat. At Dieppe they carried her luggage onto the ferry. As it was a warm night and the sea was calm, she installed herself out on deck.

"One of the Polish officers joined me and spent the entire crossing describing the sky and the stars to me in flawless French."

In the morning, for the third time in a little over two years, Paulette alighted in Victoria station. This time she wasn't met by Keith; still not called up, he'd found a teaching job. Instead, his father was waiting on the platform and he watched on while each of the Polish officers in turn kissed Paulette's hand as they took their leave. The things foreigners get up to, he must have thought.

Until it was time to go to Bradford, Paulette stayed with Frank and Daisy in Southall. Keith was no longer living with them. His makeshift home was Hounslow College, a school staffed largely by pacifists and the odd communist, and where he was teaching French. During the week he bedded down on a classroom floor and came back to Southall only at weekends. But as his anti-war views had strained relations with his parents, often he preferred to stay at no. 50 Trinity Road, where other pacifists were living.

A little before term began, Paulette took the train to Bradford. She'd been warned that conditions would be really grim up there in the dark and dour north. So the soot-laden rain that welcomed her wasn't a surprise. What was, however, was that from the very start she knew she felt at home. On the first day of term, she sensed she'd be happy at her grammar school. She was right. She was accepted for the person she was without regard for what country she came from. Her colleagues were welcoming, and the imaginative way they went about their teaching and dealt with their pupils was something wholly new to her, accustomed to the much more rigid French system. And Miss Hook, the headmistress, was as unstuffy as her staff. In the first week of term she invited Paulette to afternoon tea, an informality unheard of in France. When Paulette presented herself at the door, it was Miss Hook herself who greeted her, not a maid, and promptly asked her guest to set out the cups and plates. She wouldn't let Paulette make the pot of tea, however. That was beyond the French.

Paulette received plenty more social invitations from her colleagues, especially the younger ones. They'd gather in one another's flats to talk, discuss, argue, like the sort of student she'd not been in Aurillac. At weekends, they'd go into the centre of town or to Leeds for afternoon tea followed by the cinema. And when the weather allowed, they'd cycle onto the moors, which Paulette knew something about only from literature.

"It was just as romantic as *Wuthering Heights*. I hoped Heathcliff might come striding over the next hill!"

At two hundred miles distance, it wasn't easy for Paulete to pursue her relationship with Keith. Neither of them was sure how to proceed. At some point in summer, Paulette decided to go down to Hounslow to thrash things out. The two took a picnic to Richmond Park and talked for several hours. Even though Paulette already knew she could stay on in England if she accepted the contract Miss Hook had offered her for the next academic year, they came close to calling it a day. Paulette returned to Bradford to weigh her options and play for a little more time. But as she was doing so, on 25th June, Germany overran France. The northern half of the country passed directly under German rule, but the southern so-called *zone libre* was free only in name under the collaborationist government of Maréchal Pétain. Technically, therefore, Paulette was now a citizen of an enemy state. The prospect of internment on the Isle of Man seemed very real. It didn't happen. For whatever diplomatic reasons, she was allowed to continue at Bradford Grammar School. She didn't argue. Life went on and she continued to enjoy it. She improved her skills as a teacher, and in her spare time socialised with her friends and colleagues. They went to the Corn Exchange to hear the Halle Orchestra; they attended J.B. Priestley's famous lectures and saw his plays at the Civic Theatre. Still as insouciant as she'd been in Spain, Paulette paid little attention to such details as curfew hours. She was able to escape sanctions only because her local bobby, like her *sereno* in Madrid, took a shine to her. He warned her she'd be in big trouble if she went on ignoring the curfew. She did, but he went on only issuing warnings.

Matters did get serious one night, but not because of the curfew. This time it was an air-raid warning. Paulette was tucked in her flat, tucked up in bed when the siren went. She didn't stir. In the event, no bombs fell, but next morning her landlady went to the police to report that the foreign woman in the flat upstairs had refused to come down and could have been up to something. Maybe sending radio messages, or semaphoring with the table lamp. A police officer was sent to interrogate Paulette. She swore that she'd been fast asleep and hadn't heard the siren. As a result she was made to report to the police station twice a week. It was even put to her, in all seriousness, that she should go to London and join General de Gaulle's band of Free French. She didn't. She stayed in

Bradford and completed her year at the Grammar School, with only the twice-weekly inconvenience of signing a register.

*

On 22nd November 1940, in Southall, a truly dreadful blow befell the Sorrells. There are varying accounts of what happened. At either six or nine in the evening, a German bomber which may have strayed off course dropped a bomb as it passed over Southall. The bomb landed on the Sorrell's house, no. 6 Cambridge Road. It crashed through the roof, but I'm not certain whether or not it exploded. Again, it's not clear how much of the house was destroyed. In one account, the whole house went; in another, the front section survived. No other house, not even those immediately either side, was affected. But Keith's father was killed on the spot, and his mother critically injured. Rescuers found her in the kitchen in her chair, unconscious. She was rushed to St Mary's Hospital, Paddington, but died the next day. The couple been alone in the house with their cats. One called Peter was killed; the other, a tabby called Squibby, survived. In the letters Keith wrote subsequently to his sister Maureen in Blackpool, to which her government department had been evacuated, he gave reports of Squibby's progress, a topic of concern. One week it went to a neighbour, the next to a friend, finally to a cats' home.

I've heard two accounts of where Keith was when the bomb fell. One says that he'd gone to a meeting of pacifists in central London, had stayed the night on someone's floor and, on his way back to Trinity Road the next morning, had wanted to look in on his parents. He put his key in the front door, walked through the sitting room, opened the kitchen door and found a void. The meeting of pacifists may well be true; the rest of the story is absurd. But it's what I remember hearing when I was small. The second account is more plausible. It says that Keith had been in the house with his parents that Friday afternoon, and had slipped out to buy an evening paper. He'd heard the plane and taken cover. When the coast was clear, he'd gone back to Cambridge Road to find a crowd gathering, and when an ambulance took his parents away, he'd followed it to St Mary's Hospital, and sat with his mother until she died.

He had the good sense to ask a friend of Paulette's in Bradford to break the news to her as gently as possible. The friend took Paulette out for a walk, and chose her moment to say that "they both went". As Paulette was expecting to hear that Keith had at last received his call-up papers, she assumed that "they both" were Keith and his friend and colleague at Hounslow College, John Barker, and that where they "went" was to their Tribunals, and from there to prison. The subject was dropped for the rest of the walk. She wasn't told the truth until the next day.

*

Five pieces of paper – a newspaper cutting, a letter, two documents and one government form – are our only mementos of Frank and Daisy Sorrell. First, the newspaper cutting:

BURIAL.

Nov. 28th. Frank Herbert and Daisy Ada Alice Sorrell.

No one could help feeling the greatest sympathy for the son and daughter of Mr. and Mrs. Sorrell, of Southall, who lost their lives through enemy action. They loved Corscombe, and for some years had spent their annual holidays here. Their children respected the express wish of their parents that they should be buried in our Churchyard and so their remains, after cremation, were interred here in one grave. Many sympathising friends attended the Service.

Second, the letter of condolence to Keith from Frank's employers:

GREAT WESTERN RAILWAY,
BOARD ROOM,
PADDINGTON STATION, W.2

17th December, 1940

Dear Sir,

The Directors have learnt with profound regret that on the occasion of a recent air raid both your father and mother lost their lives.

Your father had a splendid record of thirty-five years efficient service to his credit and it is known that he was held in the highest esteem by his colleagues and superiors alike.

I desire to take the earliest opportunity of conveying to you the sincere sympathy of the Board in the great bereavement which has befallen you.

Your very truly,
Charles Hambro

As for the two documents, they look and feel like parchment. When you unfold them, they crackle and snap. They were issued in Llandudno by the Principal Probate Registry of His Majesty's High Court of Justice. A seaside resort seems quite the wrong address for the High Court. But presumably it had been evacuated, like much of the Civil Service. The violent deaths of Frank and Daisy are recorded, inevitably, in the most neutral of terms. I find it poignant that the estate passed from husband to wife for the duration of just one day. The gross value, with duty payable and interest added, is given as £922. 11s. 1d. On the back page I count eight official stamps and authenticating signatures by, among others, the GWR Salaried Staff Widows & Orphans Pension Society, the Post Office Savings Bank, and the London Co-Operative Society Limited.

Some years after his parents' death, notification was sent to Keith that final settlement of a claim made under the War Damage Act 1943, Part II, Private Chattels Scheme could be obtained on presentation of Payable Order No. Z429857 (now lost). The sum was £143. 16s. 10d. net. That is £90. 7s. 9d., amount outstanding; £15. 0s. 2d., interest; £6 15s. 0d., income tax deduction; and £43. 3s. 11d., supplementary payment. The standard rate of tax had been applied, 9s. 0d in the £.

These details are given on a scrap of badly-faded perforated paper issued by The Board of Trade (OP/1) from Jersey Road, Osterley, Isleworth, Middlesex. By calculating from the £15. 0s. 2d. interest, I'm guessing the Order was issued in 1947. I'm also guessing that the down payment on the house Keith had bought the year before would have been offset by this inheritance. Then I think again, no, half of it only, I'm certain Keith would have made sure Maureen got her share.

The violent death of his parents did nothing to change Keith's pacifist beliefs. When a few days after the funeral, his call-up papers finally arrived, summoning him to a medical, he ignored the advice of friends that he should induce an asthma attack and arrive gasping for breath. That would be bound to get him an exemption. But Keith didn't do things that way. He'd remain scrupulously honest. He'd say exactly why he'd refuse to attend the medical. He'd do so again when he received the second summons, and accept that he'd have to face a Tribunal.

I went to the office of the Peace Pledge Union a few years ago to find out more about conscientious objection. I was shown various documents; I read the clear and simple reasons objectors gave for refusing to bear arms. I also read the powerful Quaker document *The Way To End War*, written around the time of the First World War, when objectors suffered most dreadfully. I asked how Keith's Tribunal would have gone. That depended; some panels were thorough and thoughtful, but many were not. They could even descend into black comedy, the jovial PPU man told me. We had some fun sketching a scenario:

TRIBUNAL: Mr Sorrell, will you report for your medical examination?
KEITH: Absolutely not.
T: Absolutely not, *sir*.
K: Absolutely not.
T: Do you refuse to bear arms?
K: Yes.
T: Yes you refuse or yes you'll bear arms?
K: Yes I won't.
T: Or no you will?
K: Yes I refuse; no I won't bear arms.
T: Will you undertake alternative work?
K: Absolutely not.
T: Work on the land?
K: No.
T: Ambulance Corps?
K: No.
T: Are you an absolutist then?
K: Absolutely.
T: Prison it is.

The punishment for an absolutist normally was around two months imprisonment. The policy was to lock him up just long and unpleasantly enough to make him change his mind the next time. Two months confinement was nothing, of course, compared with what objectors faced in the First World War, when three years hard labour in prisons as harsh and remote as Dartmoor was normal. So were attacks by fellow inmates, while warders looked the other way. The objector might have been deliberately half-starved; he might have endured solitary confinement and even mock execution.

Keith was sent to Brixton prison in December, at the height of the Blitz. I had only the vaguest idea of how he fared there until I went to see his sister Maureen a few years after his death and she gave me the seven letters he wrote to her in

Blackpool. I'm re-reading those letters now. Keith is a remand prisoner, no. 6035, awaiting sentence. He's been given a cell in the worst spot, up on the fourth floor, where the effects of the almost-nightly bombs falling on the nearby docks are most frightening. Each time one explodes the cell shakes and his bed "dances up and down". He finds that time goes by very slowly, but old lags tell him it will pass more quickly once he's been sentenced and knows how long he's got. Conditions will ease too. So much the better. Remand prisoners are locked in their cells for much of day, and aren't allowed to work or do activities. That, Keith writes, is the worst of it. That and the cold. But although Maureen finds him "pretty miserable" on one visit, he re-assures her that "except for a few bad moments" he's in good heart, and is cheered by the kindnesses of friends who've bought him a tie, some handkerchiefs and a pair of underpants. He's grateful to Maureen for the cakes and books she's brought him. And he's struggling to come to terms with his parents' shocking death. He remembers little details about them, how his father was a real child at heart who "loved to play *Murder* at parties". He misses them terribly. He doesn't think life can ever be the same now that they've gone.

"It all seems so silly, doesn't it? War has hit us very hard, and we who always knew it was wrong! Mum and Dad have known death and I am sure we are not afraid to share it with them."

From the dates Keith mentions I work out that sentence was passed on him just before the New Year, probably 30th or 31st December. Because, on the 28th, he tells Maureen not to send any more parcels as they won't reach him. Nor will he be allowed visitors after 1st January. He doesn't know where he'll serve his term. He hopes he'll be released by the end of January, but if not, "it cannot be more than six months! A consoling thought!" Thoughts of marriage are in his mind, but they don't seem to be any consolation. He asks Maureen:

"Do you think getting married would bring us comfort? I should think it would only add to our woes!"

On 3rd January, he's still in Brixton. It hasn't been decided which prison to send him to, but it could be anywhere. For the time being, he's transferred to the Aliens' section, better than his previous cell in every way except for the bed, which may have danced up and down but was more comfortable than the mattress on the floor he sleeps on now.

The anxiety he's feeling comes through clearly, anxiety about organising his parents' grave, about solicitors and the estate. He's concerned about Paulette. Her four visits have left her distressed. He's suggested she could take Squibby back to Bradford, but thinks she wouldn't cope with a nervous cat on the train. He's worried about his own future. He knows that at least he can go on teaching and bedding down in Hounslow College when he's released. Above all, though, Keith is concerned for his sister. He tries to be encouraging. Maureen must look to the future and try to be optimistic. Before long they'll be able to rescue what remains of their parents' furniture from the "filthy store" it's in. They'll be eligible for re-housing in Southall until the family house in Cambridge Road has been rebuilt.

"So we must keep cheerful, sister, in spite of everything."

Not one of Maureen's replies to Keith has survived. What has, though, is the letter she wrote to me in 1999, a few days after she'd given me the letters from Keith. Her own letter is full of regrets:

"I'd like to think I would see my parents again and of course Keith," she writes, "but I wonder. It's so long since I've seen my parents. I feel cheated and bitter about my parents' death, even after all these years, and I believe Keith felt similarly. My dad was only 52, and my mum was only 50. They never saw Keith and me married, or their grandchildren. My mum loved boys and would have been delighted with five grandsons and a pretty little granddaughter."

Maureen misses Keith badly. She's grateful that he has a commemorative bench in Corscombe churchyard. That's where she'd like to end up, though she expects it'll be too complicated to arrange, so she'll settle for having her ashes scattered there instead. Corscombe was always the family's spiritual home. And then there's Squibby and his nine lives, since obviously he survived the cats' home.

"If you come across any mention of my mum's cat Squib, I'd be interested to know what happened to him. I know your parents had him in Twickenham, but I think he eventually disappeared. I can't think why I didn't ask Keith about him. Not that it really matters now, but I just wonder about him, when I think about it all. P.S. One thing you can answer. Why does your family call Marianne Micou? Marianne is such a pretty name."

Keith was released from Brixton in late January 1941 and went back to Hounslow College. Paulette continued to come down from Bradford at weekends, and at the end of the school year came to Middlesex to be with Keith and possibly to work alongside him, as Hounslow College quickly offered her a job. They were keen to have her. She'd be free to teach any subject she chose, not only French. She wavered. Hounslow College was an all-boys school. The girls of Bradford were one thing, but how would she control a classroom of boys, young men really, twice her size, and she barely five foot tall in her high heels!

"Well, if anybody asks," said Keith, "say you're five foot four."

She decided to take the job, and in fact had no problem with the boys. They were polite and well behaved. She was, as she said, "quite a hit". Being French and female was an asset. The one person she *did* have a problem with, ironically, was her head of department – Keith. He was worried by her method of teaching.

"He'd learnt French the proper way. He knew his grammar inside out. I couldn't really explain it to the boys. And I didn't care about things like accents. I left them out where they were meant to be and put them in where they weren't. So Keith sat me down after classes and made me learn all the rules."

*

Madame et Monsieur Pierre TOURDES vous font part du mariage de leur fille PAULETTE avec Monsieur KEITH SORRELL, Professeur de Français à Londres.

En raison des circonstances, le mariage a eu lieu dans l'intimité à Londres, le 20 Septembre 1941.

Toulouse, 13, rue Sainte-Ursule.

The formal notice, handsomely printed on a buff-coloured card, was sent by Mitoune and Pitou to friends and acquaintances to inform them of the wedding in London of Keith and Paulette. It had taken place *dans l'intimité*, quietly, intimately. *En raison des circonstances*, because of the circumstances – war of course, but also what few knew, that Paulette was three months pregnant.

The ceremony was at Brentford Registry Office on a Saturday morning when the couple had no classes to teach. In their workaday clothes, they cycled to Brentford from the flat they'd rented together in Twickenham. Attended only by the headmaster of Hounslow College and his wife, the formalities were brief. Back out on the pavement, the four of them decided on lunch in Richmond. The newlyweds took to their bicycles, the headmaster and his wife to their tandem. They found a restaurant, sat down and ordered wine. Toasts were proposed, glasses raised. As the wine was white, Paulette suggested fish to start. When that had been consumed, the waitress was summoned. What she brought, however, was not the menu they'd expected but the bill. They'd forgotten that rationing allowed them only one course. They could have done the trick of finding a second restaurant for a main course and a third for a pudding. Instead, the headmaster and his wife invited Keith and Paulette back to their house and there they all enjoyed a wedding breakfast of bread and butter and jam, sponge cake and a cup of tea.

Two days later, Keith and Paulette were back in Hounslow College. They couldn't really be spared, and they themselves didn't want a honeymoon. Both of them born teachers, they were happiest in the classroom, the Sixth Form in particular. As Keith and Paulette were only a few years older than these young men, bonds were formed, some of which endured after everyone had left Hounslow. (Twenty years later, one of those ex-sixth-formers would come to my rescue when I was going through a bad patch at university. Francis Madison, by then Director of Oxford's Museum of the History of Science, drove me out to Boars' Hill where he and his wife had a lovely house. They'd feed me, take me for walks in the country, then return me in late evening to my college.)

Through the winter of 1941–42, Paulette had two jobs. She'd added evening classes at Isleworth Polytechnic to her day-time employment at Hounslow College. It was a demanding regime, especially in view of her pregnancy, but the money was essential. Paulette stuck at it right through to the day she was taken to a nursing home in Strawberry Hill where after several hours' excruciating labour I was born. Before long, however, my mother was back in the classroom. She'd deposit me every morning in a crèche, full of guilt because apparently I was far from happy there. But as Keith's cat-and-mouse with the army went on, it was Paulette who had to top up the funds and look after their infant. It went on this way for over two years. When Keith was in prison – the number of times and the dates are far from clear – Paulette had to face the world and the war alone. She told me she lost count of the times she had to rush me down to the air-raid shelter when the siren sounded. Ah yes, I told her, I had one clear memory of that shelter. Impossible, she said, given the age you were. No, I said, the raids went on until I was two, so surely it was possible. What I think I remember is a dungeon lit by a couple of candles and smelling of earth, somewhere near the Thames. My mother and I are sitting on a bench with several other people. Everyone is silent, waiting for the explosion. When it comes the shelter shakes, the candles flicker and – this is my clearest memory – from the shelf in front of us I watch a bottle of milk fall to the ground and land upright without breaking or spilling a drop.

The stress of living with war was increasing. Paulette's nerves were more and more stretched. She held out until the V-1s, the infamous doodlebugs, appeared. There'd been nothing before so terrifying.

"We'd hear them and panic that their engine would cut out directly above us. One night that's exactly what happened. I grabbed you, *titi*, and dived under a table, but the explosion was a few streets away, thanks heavens. We were unhurt but still I went to pieces."

Keith decided that Paulette should take herself and me far from London. Blackpool was the obvious choice as Keith's sister Maureen was still there and he thought she'd be a support. We arrived during the week the Allies began their push to retake France. Where we stayed that first night, I don't know, but I do know it wasn't with Maureen, who was either in a boarding house or still at the Warwick Hotel, where she'd been when Keith was writing to her from Brixton. Either way, she'd not have been in a position to offer us a bed or even a floor. I hope there wasn't anything more to it than that, although the two women weren't close; they were so foreign to each other. Maureen had always been wary of Paulette, and she may have been remembering the forlorn lines Keith had written her from prison about the woes he feared marriage must bring. Did Maureen think he'd been proved right?

We stayed in Blackpool for two months. On leaving, we didn't head back to Twickenham. Keith had softened his position at his latest Tribunal and accepted to do agricultural work, for the sake, I imagine, of money and family stability. Which is why Paulette and I made our way to a farm in the New Forest where Keith was already at work, and having a hard time of it. The farmer was no friend of *conchies*, and he set out to make our life as miserable as possible. Keith was given the heaviest and dirtiest jobs and was allowed very little time off. Paulette had her hands full with a rotting, leaking labourer's cottage to run. I too had become a handful, scampering about, going where I wasn't meant to, including, it seems, a chicken coop patrolled by a murderous cockerel twice my size which one day went for me, in a flurry of wings talons first. My mother heard my screams and came to my rescue wielding a broom. That little monster's comb fluttering like a flag of war still pops up in my nightmares from time to time.

Paulette was pregnant again. One afternoon in January 1945 she went into a nursing home in the village with the delightful Gallic name of Dibden Purlieu, and on the 12th, Micou was born. Keith took me there to fetch mother and daughter, but did so without the permission of the farmer, which gave him the excuse he'd been looking for to sack Keith. We had the last laugh, however. With perfect timing, a letter arrived from the War Commission to tell Keith that we were to be re-housed in Southall. We'd been allocated a flat. At the end of January, our cases were piled into Micou's pram, Micou went into Paulette's arms, and I trailed behind Keith along the road to Sway station and the London train. By the evening, we were under our new roof at the top end of Lady Margaret Road, where Southall morphs into Northolt. The flat was in fact a maisonette, one of a row on the first and second floors of a redbrick commercial block. Below were a grocer, a butcher, a fishmonger, a chippie, a stationer, a chemist. For the second time in her life, Paulette would be living over a shop.

5

Giant Steps

It's the morning of 10th June 2016 and I'm on my way back to Exeter after an overnight stay in London. But first, I'm going to visit Southall, which is why I've taken a stopping train from Paddington. I've sped through Southall station a thousand times before and seen how it's been changing. Gone, the large advertisement for Quaker Oats, which, if I'm right, had a factory nearby. Most of the other installations have been pulled down as well, leaving grass to grow among rusty tracks.

I alight at a platform remote from the line taken by my usual intercity train. This side of the station has become even more forlorn than I realised. The awnings that remain are chipped and peeling, as is the surviving Victorian wooden latticework. Now, only a wire fence keeps you from getting sucked under 125s passing at full throttle.

I leave the station and turn up Avenue Road. Cambridge Road should be the first turning on the left. It's no. 6 I'm looking for. After it was wrecked by the bomb that killed my grandparents, the house was rebuilt. At some point, Keith's sister went back to live there. When I was ten, I came to stay for a few days with her, and that's the one and only time I saw it. But today I can't find any no. 6, in fact no houses at all along the side of the street where it stood. They've been replaced by a long redbrick structure of 1960s vintage at a guess. I can't work out its purpose. A small factory maybe, a light-engineering concern? Or an extension to the telephone exchange next to it? There's hardly any point in a photo, but I take one because the message on the destination panel of the parked bus parked is appropriate: "Sorry, I'm not in service".

I continue to the corner of South Road, turn right, and find myself opposite the Himalaya Palace, an Art-Deco-Oriental hybrid that used to be a cinema. I reach The Broadway. Outside a spice shop I close my eyes, breathe deep, and for a few moments I'm back in the sounds and smells of a month spent in Kerala. I return to the present and move on to Trinity Road, where Keith lodged intermittently with his pacifist friends. It's a long straight road, terraced the length of its two sides. At the far end, across the railway line, a blue-green gas-holder glints in the sun, a helpful landmark, I imagine, for planes coming into Heathrow. The house Keith knew, no. 50, must have been extended. It's bigger than most, though equally unremarkable.

I don't linger. Where I really want to be is at the far end of Lady Margaret Road, no. 480A, the maisonette where Keith brought us from the New Forest farm in 1945. I've retained a very clear mental image of it, of the block's almost brutalist design, the shops at the front, the walkway along the back. Most of all, I remember the iron staircase up to that walkway, in my infant eyes a splendid *grand escalier*.

At the bottom of Lady Margaret Road, by the Town Hall, someone tells me I can walk to the top end in ten minutes. I choose to believe him. Fifteen minutes later, I've made it only as far as no. 104. I decide to wait for a bus. Three minutes later it's depositing me outside the building I recognise immediately. In seventy years, it hasn't changed, though the shops sell different things, mostly exotic food and used cars. Above, the only alteration I can spot is that all the windows in the maisonettes have acquired double glazing.

The shop beneath no. 480A goes by the name of The Lady Margaret Superstore. It's Asian plus a more recent Polish section. I can't recollect what the shop was selling in 1945. I don't try to find out as it's the back of the building that really interests me. I make my way round to Fresh Mill Lane, neither fragrant nor boasting a mill. In general, the area is much as I remember it, except that the outbuildings have all become car repairers. There are a dozen or so of them. But above, the maisonettes and the walkway look quite unchanged. The best news, though, is that the iron staircase is still there. I'd half-expected it to have been replaced by something concrete. And it's not unlike my mental picture, if only about a third of the size. I'd like to climb it, make it clatter and clang as I remember. But it's acquired a padlocked gate, so instead I move around, taking photos from various angles so that I can show as much of the detail as possible to Micou. One of the men working in the garage of no. 482 sees me. I realise I must look suspicious. I introduce myself and tell him my story. He's amazed that I could have lived here before he was born, even before Pakistan, his country, came into existence. He calls his associates; they're working on a very large 1980s Mercedes saloon. Its raised bonnet faces out into the sunshine, like a crocodile basking in a swamp of oil and cotton waste. Three men step out into the daylight. They tell me that all four of them are from the same family. One hands me the firm's card. I read: Mr Momin Khan, Director, Khan Auto Electrician. He asks if I'd like to go up to the maisonettes. That's why I'm here, I tell him. He unlocks the gate. The staircase is no *grand escalier*, of course, but the individual steps have the feature Micou and I have always been sure we remember: a pattern of square holes, not round ones. As I climb they ring their note somewhere below middle C. I reach the walkway, and as I look along it a new memory arrives out of nowhere. I'm in a little beige coat, riding a Triang tricycle. It's painted light blue except for the flat plate that serves as both crossbar and saddle, and is a very bright red. My feet are whirling the pedals which stick out like ears from the centre of the front wheel.

I consider knocking on the door of no. 480A, but decide not to. What would I say? That I lived here once many moons ago and that some things have changed but a lot haven't? How would that be of interest? So I leave. Halfway down, I meet the postman coming up. On those giant steps of my childhood, the reality is that he barely has room to squeeze his bag past me. I go to take my leave of Mr Momin Khan and his brothers and cousins. I ask where I might get a coffee. At no. 484, the Casa Gino. Tell them we sent you. I go round to the front, enter Gino's, order at the counter, find a seat and look about me. There are several photos of Gino on the walls. Despite the name, he looks not remotely Spanish or Italian, nor does his very English caff. The reason for so many photos is that Gino died recently, as I read in the funeral announcement. It doesn't say so, but it seems to me that everyone is invited to attend. What with this, the Khans in their garage, the shops up and down the block, I'm getting the sense of a strong community spirit. I look around me as I sip my coffee. There are five other customers. Two young Asian women are having egg and chips; a couple of middle-aged white women are going one better with eggs, chips, and beans; and an elderly white man directly behind me is finishing a plate of bread and butter as he reads the racing page of his newspaper. What, I find myself wondering, would Keith and Paulette have made of this? How would they have fitted in? For all their internationalism, they had little idea about Asia. Only in the 1970s, when Neil had become an authority on the music of India and Indonesia, did they start to take some interest, though they never wanted to travel there. How well would their ideals have held up in the Southall of today? Were they more tribal than they knew, Keith more English, Paulette more French? With the EU referendum less than a fortnight away, questions of this kind have filled my head.

It's time to head on to Exeter. I take a bus straight to the station, where I've left twenty minutes to look round properly.

It has considerable family significance, and not only because Keith's father Frank became its station-master. Frank's father-in-law Walter Peart, also a railwayman, became nationally and briefly famous for the saddest of reasons. Walter was an engine-driver for the Great Western Railway. One July afternoon in 1898 his express was speeding through Acton when the boiler of his locomotive burst. He and his fireman Harry Dean were thrown back by the steam and white-hot coals that swept through their cab. Somehow, they picked themselves up and, burnt and scalded, fought their way back to the controls, which they managed to shut off. The train came safely to a stop; no passenger was killed or injured, or even suspected anything was wrong. But Walter and Harry were rushed to St Mary's Hospital. Neither survived the night, and next day their heroism was on the front page of all the newspapers.

There's an ironical twist to the story. It wasn't Walter or Harry who stopped the train, but the new vacuum-brake system which had been activated automatically the instant things went wrong. It's not likely, though it is possible, that the two men could have saved themselves by jumping from their engine. They didn't. Without a thought for themselves, they stayed at their post.

"Never mind," said Walter to a nurse an hour before he died, "I saved my train."

*

By the autumn of 1945, one problem Keith had been fearing had become urgent. When we moved into the Lady Margaret Road maisonette, he'd gone back to teaching at Hounslow College. However, as his salary was very modest and Paulette, tied down at home with two children and a third on the way, wasn't earning anything, Keith needed to find a secure, reasonably-paid teaching post elsewhere. But he was up against a brick wall. Nobody would employ *conchies*. In the end, only one expedient was left; the family would split temporarily. Paulette would take Micou and me to live with Mitoune. She was now in Toulouse where she'd found another *pension* to manage, smaller than the *Florida* in Trouville but with room enough for us. Keith would stay behind in Southall, go on at Hounslow College, and keep applying for a better job. He'd supplement his earning at weekends by delivering coal for a local firm.

On a December morning in 1945, Paulette, Micou, and I boarded a plane at Croydon Aerodrome and flew to Paris. By the evening, we were installed in the apartment of Paulette's uncle Jacques and his wife Marcelle, and eating dinner off their fine crockery. Jacques was prospering and would prosper more, buying and selling ships for scrap in the aftermath of war. The apartment in the ninth *arrondissement* was the Paris end of Jacques' operation. Paulette, Micou and I stayed there for a few days before heading south to Toulouse. I don't have much of a memory of Jacques from that visit, but I do from the one I paid him and his wife two decades later, when they made me welcome in their Côte d'Azur property. They were a rather formal pair, and until I knew them a little better, quite intimidating. Whatever the occasion, they were always impeccably dressed, she in Parisian *haute couture*, he in double-breasted suit. His voice was surprisingly soft, feeble even, a weakness which was put down to the period in his youth when he had to tend cattle in all weathers on the high ground of Auvergne. His lungs were irreparably damaged. For all his wealth and business acumen, he was a simple man, I think, and certainly a generous one. I'm sure it was he who paid our flight from Croydon, all three of us, and our onward journey to Toulouse. And it was he who drove us in his vast black American car – a Buick, Paulette thought – to Austerlitz station and our overnight train to Toulouse.

6

Mother Tongue

The war had been over a good few months by the time we boarded our train to Toulouse, but after five years of occupation and resistance, France was on its knees. Key parts of the infrastructure were in a parlous state, none more so than the railway network. Many stretches of line which had been sabotaged by the Resistance or bombed by retreating German forces either were impassable or were under heavy repair, which explains why that night our train alternately crawled along or went like the wind. I have a clear memory that the crossing of the Loire was hair-raising. High above the water, workmen's lanterns waved us along a sliver of track slung like a tightrope between half-blown pillars. Passengers stood riveted at the windows. Every few metres, the brakes would be slammed on, and there'd be shouting and arguing until a whistle blew, a green light shone, and we crawled on a few more metres. Way below, I remember, the Loire gleamed in the moonlight. Eventually, we made it across, and accelerated away. The lighting in the compartment was dimmed except for the blue night-light in the ceiling. Everyone settled down, and the steady motion of the train at speed lulled us all to sleep.

It was the stillness and silence that awoke us a while later. Someone raised the window blind, and we saw that we'd stopped in a station, brightly lit. A loudspeaker announced, *"Ici Vierzon, ici Vierzon! Dix minutes d'arrêt."*

Vierzon. A ten-minute stop. Crews had to be changed and carriage wheels tapped. A refreshment trolley passed along the platform, tinkling its bell. People got out to buy themselves a packet of *noisettes* or a *sandwich au jambon*, or just to stretch their legs. And then it was *"En voiture! Attention au départ!"* All aboard, train departing. And we'd be back into the night, moving fast. Heads lolled onto neighbours' shoulder as we all went back to sleep.

And then, everyone was woken again by the squeal of brakes and the smell of brake dust. We were three hundred kilometres further south in the high ground near Souillac. The train was reducing speed in anticipation of another damaged viaduct. When we got there, we inched along under arc lamps and naked bulbs strung up like fairy lights. Workmen with picks and shovels stood aside to watch us pass. Whatever was below the viaduct was too far down to be seen. Again, our long train made it across, and then picked up speed. Soon, the contours of the land began to level out, and the rest of the journey to Toulouse was straightforward. As dawn broke, people got themselves ready for our arrival. Some went to the *toilettes* in the hope there'd be water in the tap to rinse their face. Others stood in the corridors smoking cigarettes.

At around breakfast time, the train drew to a halt in Toulouse-Matabiau station. We looked around, but there was no one from the family to meet us. So we made our own way – by tram, taxi, or on foot, I don't recall – to Mitoune's *pension* in Cour Sainte-Ursule, two minutes from Place du Capitole, the city's main square.

(Forty years later, I listened to Lili and my mother argue about our arrival that day. Lili claimed that not only did they have no idea when Paulette would be arriving, but that they weren't even aware of Micou's existence or mine. Of course you knew, said Paulette. I wrote you several letters. But they didn't reach us, said Lili, since you were sending them from an enemy country. They *did* reach you, Paulette answered,

70

because Mitoune replied to them. I dare say you're right, said Lili. I know I am, said Paulette, my memory works.)

Mitoune's boarding house was roomy enough to accommodate three family members from England. It was a long, thin building which ran the length of one side of the Cour, a courtyard of the sort you find tucked away in French towns and cities. In the Midi, the south, they're often picturesque, almost Arabian, shaded oases with a fountain, flowers, maybe a tree or two. But not Cour Sainte-Ursule. It was, and still is, a zone of light industry. In the centre stood a workshop that stank of urine, so I thought. In fact the smell came from the row of glass amphorae filled with ammonia for the leather that was processed inside.

As for the *pension* itself, its clientele was very different from that of the *Florida* in Trouville. There, it had been holidaymakers. Here, the lodgers had jobs. I remember two in particular because often I'd be entrusted to their care. They'd take me with them to their work. One was a tram conductress who'd let me ride all day on the no. 22, back and forth to the terminus at La Côte Pavée. The other served in a shoe shop on rue Temponières. She'd install me at the front of her shop, where I'd observe the comings and goings on the street and watch customers try on shoes.

During the years of the Occupation, the German authorities had Mitoune's *pension* under constant surveillance. Places of transit, hotels and the like needed a sharp eye kept on them. But a lot got missed. Among the visitors were a number of Lili's Jewish friends, who slipped in and out beneath the radar. I've always wondered if the Germans were turning a blind eye, since one of the regular visitors to the *pension* was a prostitute whose clients of choice were German officers. Might she have been an agent working for the Resistance? Or was she supplying the Germans information? Or both? By the time we arrived from England, she'd vanished from the scene and probably from Toulouse altogether. As soon as the occupiers had left, she'd been given the classic punishment women accused of collaboration had to undergo. After a summary trail, she'd been stripped naked, she'd had her head shaved, and with several other women had been paraded on a lorry through streets thronged with jeering crowds.

There's a legendary story of vengeance that's much closer to home:

One afternoon in September 1944, there's a knock at the front door of the *pension*. Mitoune is doing something in the kitchen, Pitou's lying on his bed, and in the sitting room a friend of Lili's, a young woman who's training to be an operatic singer, is about to practice a few arias. Mitoune opens the front door. Three men are standing there, one with a rifle over his shoulder.

"*Messieurs?*"

"*Nous cherchons Mademoiselle Rolande Rousse.*"

"*Qui?*"

They repeat: they're looking for Rolande Rousse. Mitoune repeats: who?

"*Ne faites pas l'innocente, Madame.*"

They know Rolande Rousse is often here.

Mitoune stands her ground.

"*Je ne la connais pas.*"

"*Méfiez-vous, on pourrait vous embarquer.*"

Mitoune ignores the threat of arrest.

"*Je vous assure, messieurs, je ne la connais pas.*"

The men waver, then advise her to have a good think. They withdraw, warning Mitoune that they'll be back. Mitoune closes the door, moves to a window, watches until they're out of sight, then slumps into a chair, breathing hard. She's been lying through her teeth. Rolande Rousse is the young woman in the sitting room. If she'd begun to sing or had even raised her voice those three men would have taken her away and quite possibly Mitoune and others too. Mitoune collects herself, and goes to find Rolande. She tells her she must go into hiding. A little later Lili returns, learns what's happened and makes a plan. Rolande must leave as soon as it gets dark. Lili will take her upcountry to Agen by train. From there, they'll go to Moncrabeau, where friends have a safe-house.

That, so the story goes, is how Mitoune saved Rolande's life. It's amplified and melodramatic but in essence true. At the time it occurred, about a month after the liberation of Toulouse, scores were being settled. Rolande was targeted purely for being the daughter of her father, Le Commandant Rousse. He was a passionate and vocal anti-communist who'd joined the LVF (the *Légion des volontaires français contre le bolchevisme*) and gone to Germany to fight alongside the Nazis against the Russians. Treachery couldn't go unpunished. But he'd vanished, in all likelihood killed in Eastern Europe. As his wife had also died, that left only the daughter for the

Rolande, second left, and Lili, far right. Matabiau station, Toulouse. 27th September 1945.

score-settlers, the three men most probably sent by the FFI, the *Forces françaises de l'intérieur*, the Resistance.

In the end the FFI did get her. Thinking she was out of danger, she returned from Moncrabeau to finish her musical training and launch her career. But she was arrested. I've heard two versions of how that came about. One is that a municipal employee, whose only son had joined the Resistance and been killed in an ambush, wanted revenge and wasn't fussy about how to get it. He knew all about Le Commandant Rousse, and when he learnt that the daughter was back in Toulouse, he tracked her down to the *pension*. It was he who came knocking at Mitoune's door, not three FFI. The other version has it that when Rolande landed the big soprano role in an opera at the Théâtre du Capitole, a rival denounced her and got the part. Rolande was locked up in the Saint-Michel prison and then appeared in court on who knows what charge. Her trial took little time. The case against her was demolished by the lawyer hired by the Sommabère family, the good Samaritans who'd sheltered her in Moncrabeau. Rolande was acquitted, and that, for her and everyone in the *pension*, marked the true end of the war.

*

The move from Aurillac to Toulouse had made Pitou docile and co-operative, to everyone's surprise. One theory was that the presence of blonde Rolande and curly-haired Micou calmed him. His eccentricities did persist, but he toned them down. There was no more buttonholing people in streets and cafes, and he was sensible enough not to shout abuse at German soldiers. His pistol, if he still owned it, stayed hidden. Indoors, though, he was as dotty as always. Paulette remembered, for example, his theory that tortoises were endowed with as much intelligence as sheepdogs, and could be taught to behave like them. He set about training his with shouted commands and whistles. And then there were the strangest food fads. One week, he'd eat almost nothing but walnuts; the next, apples; the third, water-cress.

But he did play a practical part in the household. He had specific tasks, which he performed diligently. The one I heard about concerned vegetable peel. Quantities of vegetables were shipped to Germany every day, but bins of peel were dumped on Place du Capitole. Pitou made sure he was among the first there each morning to collect a share. He'd get up in the dark and be at the Capitole ready before anyone else for the delivery trucks. Occasionally there'd even be oysters, apparently not to German taste.

Despite the worry about Keith and jobs, the months we spent in Toulouse were a happy time for Paulette. She enjoyed being back where her student days had begun. The city was as interesting as she remembered it before the war. What's more, it was easier than she'd feared to be with her parents and sister again. I wonder, too, if it felt a relief to be back living in her mother tongue. Her situation has made me wonder what 'bilingual' really means. Does a 'bilingual' brain think in one language only – the mother tongue – and almost instantly make a translation? I put these questions to Micou recently. Apart from English, she knows three languages extremely well. She might be called quadrilingual. As she lived for ten years in Munich and Hamburg, I asked her specifically about German. Her answer was unambiguous and surprising: when she was in Germany, she thought in German. And when she was in France, the same went for French, and when in Spain, for Spanish.

What Micou said reminded me of something in my second year at Oxford. The Psychology Department had put a notice up in the Modern Languages Faculty where I went for lectures. Students who spoke English and French equally well were invited to take part in an experiment. It was simple and would take only a few minutes. As the reward was a handy two shillings and sixpence, I presented myself. I was asked to sit at a console and don a pair of earphones. I'd hear English in one ear, French in the other. All I had to do was listen. Was that it? Yes, just listen. So I did. After twenty seconds, it dawned on me that I was hearing the same text in two languages. I said so to my controller, who clicked her stopwatch. I'd completed the task. Whatever the experiment's aim was, I hope at least it took the understanding of bilingualism a step further.

*

Five months into our stay in Toulouse, Neil was born. On 29th May, to be exact, in a clinic on Cours Dillon, near the river Garonne. Three days later, when Paulette and baby were back in the *pension*, it dawned on someone that the birth hadn't been registered. Lili dashed off to the *Mairie* to tell them of Neil's arrival. But the law required births to be declared within forty-eight hours, and seventy-two had passed. Fortunately, Lili found the right man, a clerk wearied by a long war's worth of rules and regulations. He simply entered that day's date, 1st June. As a result my brother has a true and an official birthday, like royalty.

That was the one and only amusing story I heard Lili tell about wartime in Toulouse. We all knew about the armed men at Mitoune's door, of course, but it was only in the 1980s when Lili and I were chatting in her Paris flat one day that I got to hear others equally alarming. She told me of her arrest by a German patrol when she and a few young women were walking down rue d'Alsace-Lorraine. Some of the group were nurses who, like Lili, were in uniform. One, Arlette, was tall, blue-eyed, and ash-blond. All the others were small and swarthy. A German patrol noticed them and became suspicious. They stopped them. *"Papiers!"* Your papers. Identity documents were scrutinised, photos compared with faces. They were satisfied with all except Lili. The others were let go, and she was taken to police headquarters. Checks were made, Mitoune was telephoned as well as other people Lili named. It took time, but in the end the police had to accept that Lili was exactly who she said she was. She was not Jewish, and

Lili. Toulouse. Circa 1941.

her papers were in order. Released, she rushed off in search of tall, blond, blue-eyed Arlette. Jewish Arlette.

Lili got Arlette to the same people who'd sheltered Rolande in Moncrabeau. Other friends weren't so lucky. Poor Annette, for example, who was seized in a *rafle*, a round-up, and taken first to the Caffarelli barracks and then with scores of others to a train of cattle-trucks in a yard outside Matabiau station. There they were left for three days with only such food and water as the charities and the Quakers could bring. Lili was working with the Quakers and, when she found out where Annette was, she made her way to the railway yard. At the entrance, a German soldier thrust his rifle across her chest to stop her going any further. He looked worn out, Lili remembered. She tried to explain that as a Quaker she had the right to visit the prisoners in the train. The soldier pushed his rifle even more firmly against her. "*Raus! Raus!*" he shouted, and when Lili persisted, he pointed his rifle at her. Suddenly she understood. He knew that if she went inside the yard, with a face like hers, she'd could easily have wound up with Annette en route to a concentration camp.

"*Je dois ma vie à cet homme.*" She owed her life to that man.

Annette survived, but only just. For several days and nights, her cattle truck – designed for eight horses or seventy men, *8 Chevaux 70 Hommes*, to echo the title of an account of the deportation train that was shunted round France for weeks until those locked inside started to die – took her eventually to Ravensbrück. She survived and eventually made it back to Toulouse. By then, she was a walking skeleton. She told of how she'd avoided starving to death by stealing scraps of the leather she stitched onto army uniforms, plus a few drops of sewing-machine oil, and boiling them up later to make herself a meal. Now, her health was damaged beyond repair, and she died not many months later.

Lili supplemented these stories with large glasses of Bordeaux and the cigarettes I'd brought her. I asked her about other stories I knew only vaguely. I'd heard something about two cousins, Zézé and Pierre. They'd been of an age to fight in the war, but hadn't. So why was that? Were they in the Resistance? No, said Lili, soon after France fell they were both packed off to Germany in the S.T.O., the *Service de Travail Obligatoire*. Slave labour, in effect. They spent the war working in a steel factory. The conditions were dreadful, the food meagre. Zézé was a strapping youth and survived undamaged. Not so Pierre, who from birth had been thin and sickly. I met him once, when I was about ten, and I remember a hollow-chested man who wheezed and coughed. His lungs were wrecked, and he died young.

Then Lili told me the best story of all, a black comedy about a British airman, a Polish spy and a German officer, all of whom were in the *pension* at the same time one evening. The airman was on the run. In the morning, he'd be heading for the Pyrenees, which he'd cross on foot aided by a *passeur*, a local guide. Once in neutral Spain he'd be able to get back to Britain. Now he was asleep in the corridor, and visible to anyone who happened to pass. In a room to the left, the Pole was playing gramophone records very loudly to drown the sound of the messages he was radioing. And in the boudoir to the right, the German officer was enjoying the company of the prostitute who may or may not have been an agent. When in due course the German officer made his way back along the corridor to the front door, he neither investigated the airman asleep on the floor nor the suspiciously loud music coming from inside the radio operator's room.

"It sounds like pure fiction," I said to Lili. "You're very lucky that it didn't end badly. What a war, so much worse for you than it was for us in England."

"Oh no, on the contrary," said Lili. "At least we knew our enemy, we saw him every day, almost like a neighbour. We learnt how to deal with him. You didn't."

Only years later, after her death, did I hear from Paulette the most poignant and personal of Lili's stories, a story Lili never herself told. There was in Toulouse a well-known and respected family called Lévinettre, brilliant, charming and successful people all. The two sons, Robert and Etienne, were talented and ambitious, destined it seemed to go far. Lili was in love with one of them, and the other was in love with her. Which was which, I don't know. But as they were Jewish, when the war came Lili helped Etienne to disappear into a Resistance network. Robert was not so fortunate; he was seized in a *rafle*. On his way to Drancy – the holding-camp in the northern suburbs of Paris, from which inmates were sent to Germany – he wrote a letter and threw it from the train. Against the odds, it reached Toulouse and came Lili's way. Paulette didn't know what that letter said, but it was the last that was heard of Robert. He must have ended up in Germany and died in an extermination camp. Lili never married.

*

A few weeks after Neil was born, news reached Paulette that at last Keith had found a job, and an excellent one at that: head of languages at Steyning Grammar School for Boys, in a lovely part of the country, West Sussex. The headmaster had no problems with pacifists, it seemed.

And so, on an August evening, Paulette, Neil and I boarded the night train to Paris and then went on to England, leaving Micou behind. A couple of weeks later, Lili would bring her directly to our new home in Steyning.

The journey up to Paris was less nerve-wracking than eight months earlier. The track, bridges and viaducts had largely been repaired. Paris to Dieppe was straightforward too, as was the Channel crossing. Almost twenty-four hours after leaving Toulouse, Paulette hauled Neil, me and our luggage off the train at Victoria station, where there was a man waiting for us.

He waved, approached, embraced my mother and took my baby brother from her arms. Then he turned to me and kissed me. I winced. By what right was he doing that? And what was he saying to me? I couldn't understand a word. Who was he anyway?

"*Dis bonjour à ton papa*," said Paulette.

Say hello to your father.

7

Listen with Mother

On a day I hope for Keith's sake was free of rain, a lorry was cleaned up and loaded with furniture instead of the usual coal. As Keith hadn't yet learnt to drive, the owner, who was his weekend employer, had agreed to haul our possessions down to our new home. There were no passenger seats in the cab, so with Neil in her arms and me in tow, Paulette made the journey from Southall to Steyning by bus, tube and train. To keep an eye on the furniture, Keith rode the fifty miles in an armchair strapped to the flat bed of the lorry, and arrived if not soaked certainly cold.

No. 25 King's Stone Avenue stood in the middle of a row of five small houses. The setting was semi-rural, at the eastern edge of Steyning. Behind our long meandering road – prefabs, terraces, bungalows, villas – was meadowland bisected by the River Adur (which Paulette decided was sinister; it gave her *the willies*). Beyond was Truleigh Hill on which stood radio masts whose lights gave me a sense of security in bed at night, the way the blue night-light had on the Toulouse train.

The first part of our life as a re-united family coincided with two social reforms that brought us all enormous benefits: the Butler Education Act and the National Health Service. While the new education system would always be contentious; the NHS was seen wholly as a good: free doctors, free hospitals, free medicine for a country rebuilding itself after a devastating war. Ironically, in terms of nutrition, the health of the nation was better in the war and the 1950s than ever before – or since. Forced by circumstances, we found ourselves eating the right amounts of the right food. The wartime "Dig for Victory" ethos endured into the peace. A lot of people went on growing much of their own food in their gardens or on allotments. The back gardens in King's Stone Avenue had very few lawns or flower-beds. Everywhere it was vegetables: neat rows of onions and cabbages and Brussels sprouts on their thick stalks, and fragile-looking bamboo wigwams that supported peas and runner beans. Micou, Neil and I, like most children, ate a good amount of vegetables every day, willingly or not. Carrots, cabbage, peas, tomatoes were easy, but parsnips, turnips and swedes were a battle. Potatoes were the favourite, and Paulette would put dollops of creamy mash on our plate to help with the very fatty meat we weren't allowed to leave. To set the example, Keith would cut a chunk of fat and make a big show of chewing it with exaggerated pleasure. He insisted that it was the best thing on our plates, and I think he believed it. We children resisted until a compromise was reached: two forkfuls each. That meat was on par with the cod-liver oil we had to take every morning. Paulette had a struggle to get it down our throats. *Pour la bonne volonté,* she'd say, show some good will, a bit of good grace. The reward was a spoonful of the orange juice which, like the cod-liver oil, was issued free to young families, and which we went on the bus to collect from a dispensary in Storrington.

And when I started primary school, there was the free milk, the daily third of a pint for every child. From our classroom in the Primary School we'd hear the whir of the electric float, the clunk of the motor cutting out, then the chink-chink of glass as the crates were manhandled across the playground. The bottles would be distributed by the milk monitors. Once we'd drained them, we'd replace them in their crates and give the cardboard tops to our teacher to be brought out in the afternoon for us to weave with cotton thread and raffia in a soporific atmosphere of radiators, floor polish and jam-jars full of sticky buds.

Our National Health doctor was a South African with a huge domed forehead. I don't know if Dr Dingemans was an anti-apartheid Afrikaner who'd wanted to quit the country, or had been forced to. I can still picture him at the desk in his surgery next to the Clock Tower, authoritative in his suit and half-moon glasses. He's uncapping his Parker 51 fountain pen to write out a prescription, which he tears off the pad and hands to Paulette. I see us crossing the High Street to take the prescription either to Mr Bligh or Mr Thompson, Steyning's two chemists.

Free health care, then, was one of the two big transformations to our post-war world; the other was the Butler Act that established universal free secondary education up to the age of fifteen. It also introduced the 11-Plus exam, which would become such a divisive issue as it did nothing for the social mobility the Butler Act should have fostered. The exam was meant to show which type of education would suit a child best: grammar, technical high or secondary modern. The trouble was that nearly everyone, pupils and parents alike, saw the grammar schools as the only goal. Children "passed" or "failed" the 11-Plus. Parents offered them rewards. In the playground we'd compare them:

"My parents are giving me a woodwork set."

"Mine are giving me a watch."

"I'm getting a train set."

"I've been promised a bike."

"So have I, but with Sturmey-Archer gears."

Those who "failed" got nothing, I suppose, and were shunted off to Steyning's new Secondary Modern on the far side of the Shooting Field council estate where they vanished from the lives of friends heading to the Grammar School.

Unless they went private, Steyning's children started their education at the primary school near Church Street. It was a gaunt building of four large rooms, an office and two cloak-rooms. It looked like a cross between a chapel and a village hall. Micou, Neil and I were enrolled at the appropriate age, but only I stayed the course and sat the 11-Plus there. My teachers were, I recall, below average. One was an ex-squad-die, a Mr Green or Brown or Black or White. He'd been drafted in the aftermath of the war when there was a desperate short-age of teachers. The fact that he was unqualified and without talent wasn't an issue. All I can remember him trying to teach us was handwriting. Morning after morning, we'd copy down the twenty-six letters of the alphabet which he wrote on the blackboard in impeccable copperplate. If there was any time left over, he'd stick a foot on his table and deliver us a sermon on the virtues of polished shoes. Had there been an iron on the premises, I'm sure he'd have removed his shirt to show us how he pressed clothes.

When the bell rang sometime after three o'clock for the end of classes, I shot off to find my mother and take her out of range before my classmates could hear her ghastly French accent. I grabbed her hand and tugged her homewards down the twitten where the stag-beetles lived.

Three and four years later, when their turn came, Micou and Neil started at the primary school. By then it had become a dan-gerous as well as unsatisfactory place. A louche teacher who crept around on thick crepe soles took a fancy to the very pretty Micou and started to molest her. Neil endured canings so fero-cious, he's told me, that the whole school stopped to listen. So our parents removed them. But where to send them? Briefly, it seems, Summerhill was in the frame. Keith very much liked the sound of A.S. Neill's experimental school, its progressive phi-losophy, its internationalist outlook. Its aim was to get children to think freely and act independently. They could choose which lessons to go to, for example, and whether or not to play sport, and even (unless that was my father's joke) when to get out of bed. They didn't wear a uniform and they called teachers by their first name. Children educated this way, so the theory went, grew up perfectly adjusted.

In the end it was the high fees that killed off Keith's dream of Summerhill. Micou and Neil transferred instead to a small private school, the two front rooms of an Edwardian villa three hundred yards from our house. In lieu of fees, Paulette gave the school a few hours per week of her time. Her brief was to teach, of all things, the English vowel system.

"With my accent, can you imagine?"

Most of the time when we weren't at school, Micou, Neil and I spent outdoors at play. Play? We went about it the way Marines train. We made sorties to the Adur and slithered down its treacherous banks; we climbed among the ruins of Brambar Castle; we abseiled down the chalk pit on the Round Hill. We'd return home cut, gashed, split-lipped, broken-boned, half-drowned. Micou fell out of a tree and broke an arm; Neil tumbled into a tank full of silage and was yanked out just in time by Farmer Barratt; and, when I managed to climb a telegraph pole and swinging like a gymnast from the bottom wire, the fire brigade had to be called to snatch me down.

Was this all just high spirits? Or something more Oedipal? Were we hoping to destroy our parents? I know that they turned to books of psychology to find out where they were going wrong. The guru of the day was Dr Benjamin Spock, but, Paulette admitted later, he led them up the garden path. We children didn't need his laissez-faire philosophy. The very opposite, in fact. What we lacked were boundaries.

Ironically, it was a bit of thoughtlessness, our parents' not ours, that brought the three of us to our senses, at least for one night. I'd woken up and seen that the lights downstairs were on when I thought they shouldn't be (it was probably around ten thirty). I went down to investigate. Keith and Paulette weren't anywhere. I raced back upstairs; their bed was empty. I shook Micou and Neil awake. We dressed, went out and ran from door to door asking for them. No one had seen them. We returned home in tears and I was preparing to go to the police station when our parents reappeared. They hadn't been very far away. But they never left us alone like that again.

Whenever I think of those years in King's Stone Avenue, it's this kind of melodrama that first comes to mind. But then come the gentler memories. There are the French nursery rhymes and songs played to us on our first gramophone: *Savez-vous planter les choux* (how to plant cabbages with your nose, ears, chin, elbows ...), or *Il était un petit navire* (a weepy story of a little boat that can't handle the open sea), or *Malbruck s'en va-t-en guerre* (the Duke of Marlborough off to war, tragically never to return). And there is my clearest memory of all, the fifteen minutes every day, Monday to Friday, when our wireless set took hold of our imaginations. Just before a quarter to two in the afternoon, we'd settle down; *Listen with Mother* was about to start. Paulette would turn a knob on the wireless and we'd watch it open its green eye as Paulette found herself a place among us on the sofa. A glockenspiel tinkled a few notes of Fauré, then:

"Are you sitting comfortably?" asked Daphne Oxenford, in her Oxenford accent.

Yes we were.

"Then I'll begin. Once upon a time ..."

And from that living box in the corner came stories, nursery rhymes, and songs until, at two o'clock, Daphne said goodbye to us, we said goodbye to her, and the green eye closed again.

At bedtime Paulette might read to us from various books. There were stories about old women who lived in shoes, and engines called Gordon and Edward and Thomas who had human faces and spoke English to one another. And there were the Tintin books Mitoune sent us from France, of which I remember, for scary reasons, only *Tintin au Congo*. The image that stays in my mind is of white-eyed, grass-skirted black men dancing around a cauldron in which they're boiling a couple of Europeans wearing pith helmets.

Beyond bedtime stories and Daphne Oxenford, I went on looking for bigger and bigger tricks to pull, until I found my boldest: I would wreck a train. I don't believe I wanted to kill anyone. Simply, I wasn't thinking of the passengers. I was doing a kind of experiment. How did a train crash go? Would it look exciting? There was a stretch of line between Steyning and Henfield where trains travelled fast across an embankment, where my experiment would be sure to succeed. There was a good drop either side of the track. Over several days, I collected stones and bricks and branches, and hid them near the line. On my chosen afternoon, I made certain no one was watching, laid my arsenal out on the rails and found somewhere safe to watch. The train appeared, going fast. It ploughed into my ambush – and straight through it. The stones and bricks and branches were pulverised or brushed aside. In dismay I watched the train disappear as if nothing had happened, as indeed it hadn't. I sloped off home. But by the evening I'd hatched a brand new plan.

I put it into action the next day. I took up a position on one parapet of the road-bridge over Steyning station. Below, the train was getting up steam, about to leave. When it did, I planned to run to the other parapet and be ready with some large stones. If I was accurate, I should be able to throw them straight down the chimney of the engine as it reappeared. I don't know what I thought I'd achieve. Perhaps the train would come to a halt; perhaps the engine would break down. And then what? The train got under way and steam enveloped the bridge. I started across but didn't make it to the other side. A lorry was passing through the steam and it ran smack into me. Once the steam had cleared, I was found lying on the ground, complaining that my arm hurt. People gathered and sat me up. Apart from the arm, it seemed I'd not been hurt. Someone took me home. Paulette opened the door, went white, gathered herself and sent for Dr Dingemans. He arrived, cleaned the cuts to my arm, strapped it up and left insisting he must be called back if I didn't settle. For a few hours all was well. But by the evening I was talking gibberish. Dr Dingemans returned, shone a light into my eyes, held up a hand and asked me to count the fingers. When I reached seven he summoned an ambulance and I was rushed to Southlands Hospital in Shoreham and X-rayed. My skull had been fractured across my forehead. It took a month for it to mend. Once I was allowed to move around, I made friends with patients on my ward, then all the others. But I got bored, and wandered about looking for more things to do. Keith and Paulette took turns to visit me. They brought the news that Micou had done herself yet another injury, and that Neil was recovering from some illness. Why didn't I write them a letter? I did:

"Dear Micou, I am so sorry that you heart your eye. I am aloud to sit up. I here that Neil was kind to you he let you look at the comic. Dear Neil, I am so glad you are better. Love from Martin."

On the day I was to be dischraged, I'd vanished. My mother feared the worst, that I was up to my old tricks by the railway. But it was a false alarm. A nurse had spotted me in the women's ward rewinding the ball of wool which had fallen from the bed of an elderly patient, and telling her all about my family and our adventures.

My fragile head kept me subdued for a while. The Christmas before my tenth birthday, deciding a lesson in self-control was overdue, my father agreed a plan with Mitoune. For some time

I'd been agitating for a wrist-watch. Plenty of boys my age had them. So Mitoune bought me one in Paris, and despatched it to my parents. A few days before Christmas, Keith produced a stylish oblong box and invited me to open it. On a bed of satin I saw exactly the sort of watch I dreamt of: it had luminous hands and embossed numerals set against a cream-white dial; the strap was made of luxurious brown leather. Put it on, Keith said. With his help, I did, then placed my arm flat on the table just to let it all soak in.

And here's where my father, who'd dealt well with all my misdeeds so far, made his big blunder. There was one thing he'd not said. The watch was not for Christmas but for my birthday, still three months away. Keith would remove the watch and I'd have to learn to wait, like a grown-up.

I couldn't wait. The following morning, I was outside the jeweller's in the High Street assessing the watches in the window. There were some as beautiful as Mitoune's, but the prices were impossible: eight, ten pounds, twelve guineas, twenty. The cheapest at £3 was a clumsy and crude Newmark with black cudgel hands on a flimsy dial, and the whole thing slapped into a case that looked like a piece of tin. There was not one thing I liked about it. But I had to have it. It was a *watch*.

My parents' desk in the sitting room was never locked. Inside were papers, deeds, insurance policies, passports, ration books. At the back was a recess that contained paper money-bags. In one, there were threepenny bits; in the second sixpenny pieces; shillings in the third; florins in the fourth; half-crowns in the fifth. There weren't too many coins in any of them, so, to remain undetected, I'd have to remove only a very few at a time over a period of several nights. When I'd reached £3, I went to the jeweller's, did the deal and left with the Newmark. Which, of course, I realised straightaway I'd never be able to wear, could never show to anyone and would have to keep permanently hidden. And there was an additional problem:

Micou and Neil knew what I'd been up to. I'd have to see if I could bribe them to keep their mouths shut.

It seems strange to me that any shopkeeper, let alone a jeweller, should do a transaction with a nine-year-old boy who's counting out £3 in sixpences and threepences. I've wondered if he was in league with Keith and Paulette and that my plot was known all along. Because the fact is the moment I got home I was "discovered". My mother questioned me and made me turn out my pockets. Knowing Keith would be home at any moment, I panicked, rushed upstairs, dived under my bed and curled up in a ball. Minutes later I heard him on the stairs. He entered my room. I watched his feet at the foot of my bed and waited to be yanked out. But my father's feet stayed rooted. Eventually he spoke, "I never thought I'd father a thief."

He didn't wallop me, I wasn't locked in my room, I wasn't gated. What my parents decided to do was as perfectly judged as my lesson in patience had been misguided. I'd repay the £3 by doing jobs of various sorts, each one individually priced. An account would be kept in a notebook which I can still see to this day: light-green covers, black spine, blue ruled lines and columns for the figures. Keith noted down each job and its value and invited me to check the sums. The tariff must have been something like this: shopping, 6d; making the beds, 6d; washing and drying up, 3d; cleaning all shoes, 6d; cleaning Raeburn and fetching coal, 6d; front-room fire and fetching coal, 6d; cleaning all windows on the inside, 9d; dusting all rooms, 6d; Ewebanking carpets 6d.

I have to hand it to my father, it was a shrewd strategy. Punishment, rehabilitation and elementary maths rolled into one. I set about my tasks eager and willing. It took me about two months to clear my debt, and from that point, Micou has assured me, I became a goodie-two-shoes.

Not quite. The thieving went on for a while, petty stuff, a few sweets snaffled from the open trays in Woolworth's

Micou, Martin, Neil. Bognor Regis. September 1954.

at Shoreham, but nothing more from home. Then even that stopped. I was experiencing new feelings, puzzling and oddly tender. I ceased to cast myself as the railway's wrecking-ball and looked for something constructive to do. I got my chance, but kept what I did a secret. At the end of a week of sneaking out after dark, I asked my mother to come with me for a walk. Intrigued, she agreed. We followed the path along the field between the church and the railway line, turned a corner, and I revealed the broken-down engine I'd been polishing night after night. We stood together in the moonlight, looking. For a few moments, my mother said nothing. When she did, it wasn't at all what I expected:

"What a funny little chap you are, darling."

8

The Terrace

Early in 1952, Paulette went through the rooms of no. 25 King's Stone Avenue with a tape-measure, sizing the furniture. Next, she cut out bits of paper to represent our cooker, chest of drawers, wardrobes, beds, tables, sofa, armchairs, dining-room chairs. She shuffled these bits of paper around the floor to give herself an idea of the lay-out of the rooms in the house we were moving to. A month later, the removals men loaded the contents of no. 25 into their lorry and unloaded them a mile away in no. 6 Southdown Terrace.

By a matter of yards, our new house was on the right side of the tracks, almost within sight of Goring Road, Steyning's grand avenue, though in social terms a mile away. At the time Southdown Terrace was built, in the 1870s, it would have been one of the town's most solid addresses, mid-middle-class. But by the 1950s it had become shabby. It was formed of eight tall, thin houses built on a slope. It was reached by a rough road of ridges and potholes. At the top, where it levelled off, stood the Railway Hotel, built in anticipation of the boom the line never managed to create. By the time we moved in, it had become a last-drink saloon.

Each house in the terrace had a patch of garden at the front, enclosed by a low retaining wall, and, if it hadn't been removed, a wooden gate. At the rear, there was a coal store, an outside lavatory and a lean-to shed. Three steps led up to the patch of earth in which some owners grew beans and carrots but others piled their junk.

By the time we moved in, the terrace had become a mishmash of social groups that included one hardly known in Steyning, foreign refugees. Three other classes were there: working-class, lower-middle-class, middle-class. Upper-middle-class and higher were missing, unless any of the refugees belonged to dispossessed European aristocracy. We saw ourselves as right in the middle of middle-class. Not Paulette, though, who insisted with undeniable logic that because she worked, she was working-class. She understood perfectly well, of course, what "working-class" meant, but the divisions and sub-divisions of the British class system angered her. She had good reason. Nowhere would Paulette be made to feel her outsider status more than in Steyning, a town probably no quicker to judgement than any other, but just the right size to make it seem it was.

During our tenure, these were the occupants of Southdown Terrace's eight properties:

No. 1 was a Polish family, Mr and Mrs Radzinski plus a daughter called Kaja. They were refugees, but I don't know when they'd arrived, nor whether Mr had been a member of one of the Polish squadrons that fought in the Battle of Britain. A man of few words, at least English ones, he spent his working day among the tomatoes, beans and lettuces in his smallholding at the rear of the terrace. When we saw him we always exchanged a greeting, and when we didn't see him it was because he was in his glasshouse boxing up chrysanthemums to load onto the train up to Covent Garden. We hardly saw the wife, though Neil remembers the flash of gold teeth when she smiled at him as he perched on her scullery window, watching her peel potatoes.

No. 2 was a mystery. Never any activity. No one ever was caught leaving or entering. A house of ghosts.

No. 3 was a family of Hungarians who arrived a while after us, presumably in the aftermath of the uprising of 1956. Because we knew nothing about them, they were more exotic than the Radzinskis, but less mysterious than the no. 2s.

No. 4 was the Atkinson clan. Upper-lower-middle-class, probably. The daughter, Maureen, was the same age as Micou, and stayed her friend until the 11-Plus separated them.

No. 5, the Tombs, the station-porter, the one who held trains for Paulette, and his wife and their many children. Five of them we knew: Les the dustman; donnish Dennis; studious Silvia; Sheila, incorruptible despite her reputation; Maggie, Neil's favourite, *a hoot*, who wanted to live in Gay Paree; and Maggie's dog Bobbie.

No. 6, us, thought by most of the terrace to be a bit racy, thanks to Paulette, and as exotic as nos 1 and 3, though more approachable since we all spoke English.

No. 7 was the Blackabys, at first. Win Blackaby was the Physics teacher at the Grammar School and a colleague of Keith's. Mrs Blackaby, Anne, was a restless soul who chain-smoked as she talked to Paulette over the garden wall. There were two children, whom we hardly saw. The Blackabys were followed by the Burgesses. Mr Burgess was a window-cleaner who towed his buckets and shammy leathers in a special cart he'd bolted to his pushbike. Of Mrs Burgess, none of us can remember a thing. Did she even exist? The daughter, Thea, certainly did. She was real alright, the neighbourhood's leading hormone-stirrer.

No. 8, the Bests. How many of them there were, what they looked like, what they did, I have no recollection. Ghosts, but as at least they had a name, more substantial than no. 2.

The near-doubling of floor space and the greater proximity to the centre of Steyning, the schools and the trains were the reasons Keith and Paulette settled for Southdown Terrace. And the cost, of course. They'd have preferred the Edwardian semi they'd viewed in Maudlin Lane but a price couldn't be agreed. So it had to be the terrace. Even so, financially it was a stretch. Not only the mortgage; repairs and improvements were needed. The sash windows had warped or rotted or both. The coal fires in the downstairs rooms heated little more than the hearth. The Raeburn in the kitchen was moody, the plumbing Heath Robinson. There was no bathroom; the redundant fifth bedroom had to be converted. The lavatory was a wooden thunder-box with a cast-iron cistern and chain high above. There was also an outside lavatory with an identical thunder-box, this one shared with spiders round the walls and insects in the bowl. Primitive arrangements on a par with France, and which I don't think we ever updated. Our lavatory paper we did though, when Bronco and Izal and emergency squares of newspaper were replaced by Velvex tissues. "Velvety Texture, Strong, Hygienic", it said in flowery letters on the purple box.

A house on three floors gave us a luxury we'd not known before – privacy. I was allocated the front attic as my bedroom, what I wanted, a cave in the sky with a window for spying on the world – and where I'd soon come close to defenestration, the night I sleepwalked out onto the roof. I remember clambering about the tiles for a few moments, managing not to slip, then sleepwalking my way back inside, but straight into the wardrobe which I mistook for my bed. I don't recall ever climbing out again. I did continue my sorties, however, and for a long time, but only indoors and only when I was fully awake. I'd creep about opening cupboards and drawers simply out of curiosity. I don't think I ever found anything of interest except two oddities lying among the underwear: a rubber tube, closed off at one end, and a jar of a jelly that might have been Vaseline. I didn't know what any of it could be for. Now that I do, I've come to think our parents meant me to discover them to save themselves the embarrassment of talking to me, or any of us, about sex.

At 8:30 on a September morning in 1953, I was almost ready for day one of my first term at the Grammar School, kitted out in blue cap, blue blazer with school crest (lion rampant, fleur-de-lis, and the date 1614), white shirt, long grey socks, short grey trousers, all supplied by Kinch & Lack of Worthing. All that remained was to fasten my tie, which I'd only half-managed. As Keith leant over me to re-do the knot, his shaving soap smelt like my introduction to the grown-up world. We left the house together, strode side by side to the school, but went in by different doors. Twenty minutes later, we reappeared in the assembly hall, I cross-legged on the floor among the new intake, he on the platform, one gowned figure among fifteen, deliberately not seeing me. Between the hours of nine and four, I'd have to forget that he and I were family. I understood that from that moment on I'd be embarrassed and even disturbed to be the only pupil in the school with a parent on the staff. This needed to be counter-balanced. I vied for the role of best class clown. I collected reprimands and clips round the ear as a matter of honour. I got myself caned once, not by my father, thankfully, but the headmaster. All my trespasses were minor. The major ones belonged to the past. I wasn't going to jeopardise my place in such an illustrious school, which I'd got into by the skin of my teeth. I'd come close to "failing" the 11-Plus exam. I was "borderline", which meant I was summoned to an interview with the headmaster, and performed well enough to be accepted into the bottom stream, exactly as would happen later to Micou and Neil.

With the men on the platform that first day of term sat two women, neither wearing an academic gown. One was the Swedish matron; her job was to look after the ninety boarders who'd been deposited by parents living abroad or in the armed forces, or who'd failed to get their boys into a public school. The other woman was the art teacher. She left soon after and was replaced by a stocky young man I remember for his motorbike and his problem with palato-alveolar sibilant fricatives, the *sh-* sounds he couldn't make without thrusting his lower lip so far forward that his bottom row of teeth showed like the mouth of an angler fish. "Go to the drawer marked *shhh*ugar paper and get yourself a *shhh*eet." Most of the staff were memorable in one way or another. There was the English teacher whose shoes curled up at the toes like a court jester's, and who read us Keats and Wordsworth unaware that his badly-extinguished pipe was scorching the pocket he'd stuffed it into; the exasperated woodwork teacher watching us manhandle plane ("leave your pencil line on the wood, boy"); the ghostly Edwardian with the Edward-Elgar moustache who failed to teach us any chemistry; the biology master who asked me when I went abroad to look for the finger he'd lost in the war. And, poignantly, the unhinged ex-university lecturer who introduced Spanish to the school and taught it brilliantly until the day he flipped, and locked himself away in his flat which he convinced himself was the cave of the Prodigious Magician in the Calderón play he was teaching us.

And then there was my father. I quickly realised I must do everything to show my classmates that I was one of them and not "Daddy's Boy". I always hung back, and did all I could in Keith's classes to make myself as inconspicuous as possible. I sat towards the back of the room, and bit by bit I accepted the irony of having him teach me my mother's mother tongue. I'm sure his methods were excellent but recall nothing about them. Neil, on the other hand, remembers how Keith devised imaginative little scenarios. He'd organise the class into rows, each one representing a province of France (where that led to next, Neil's forgotten). And then he lined up pronouns – *je, tu, il, elle, nous, vous, ils, elles* – on the blackboard in the formation of a football team, with pronouns *y* and *en* as double goalkeepers, a method that is more likely to hit the mark with teenage boys than the frankly bizarre one Keith had used a few years earlier in my friend Dave Mitchell's very first French lesson with him. Dave has told me that Keith devoted the entire forty minutes to the French vowel sounds, which he articulated with exaggerated movements of his facial muscles, and located in their correct positions on the diagram of the mouth he'd drawn on the board.

My relationship with Keith in school hours was artificial, as if we were in a theatre playing roles we'd learnt. We called each other by stage names. His was "sir", mine was "Sorrell". (Boys in those days were always addressed by their surnames.) We kept our distance and Keith was careful not to show me any special favours. But behind the formality, he always kept a watchful eye on me. We have a document in our treasure chest, one of my end-of-term reports that rather touchingly sums up our dual relationship. On one side of the sheet, K. H. Sorrell BA has entered the French mark and written an overall assessment of pupil Martin Sorrell. He's signed the report and brought it home for the pupil's parents. And the next day it's plain Keith Sorrell who reads it and on the reverse writes himself the parents' response.

*

Sometime in the late 1950s Paulette changed schools. It had gone round the grapevine that she was an outstanding teacher, adored by her pupils. Her confidence had grown; she now wanted a position somewhere more interesting, and presumably better paid, than the convent in Hove. Various schools wooed her, Roedean the best-known of them. It was difficult at first to see why Paulette should choose St Michael's, Burton Park, why a long bus ride from Steyning to Pulborough, then twenty minutes in a car (chauffeur-driven, admittedly) were preferable to the easier train journey of a few miles to Brighton and Roedean. But St Michael's offered her a bespoke deal: she could teach Spanish as well as French; she'd have a Sixth Form group; and a private flat would be made available to her. This was very attractive, of course, but what clinched it was the personality of the Lady Warden, the head-mistress. Pat Lancaster was a remarkable woman. I've looked up her obituary – she died in 2004 – which calls her one of the great educationalists of the twentieth century. Paulette found her open-minded, slow to judgement, a wonderful listener and a wise counsel, and considered her a good friend. It was a blow, then, when Pat moved on to another school and was replaced by a younger woman who sped about the county in a sports car and whom Paulette first dismissed as a "floozy". She even thought of leaving St Michael's. In the event, she stayed on for almost twenty more years, in part because the floozy turned out to be brilliant at her job.

Mainly, Paulette stayed because we needed the money. Though the family finances were improving, for the trips abroad that they wanted us to have, Keith and Paulette still needed to earn more. Keith had started already to do unpaid work for a company called Educational Travel – it organised stays and courses in Europe for British schoolchildren – and in exchange was getting discounted trips for the family. So he and Paulette got themselves taken on as examiners for a GCE Board. Keith chose to mark O- and A-Level scripts, moun-tains of them; Paulette toured schools conducting French and Spanish oral exams.

Paulette's was by far the better option. Oral exams involved little paperwork, and, in those days before the exams were tape-recorded, all she required was her ears and a notepad. By four each afternoon, it was done and out of her mind. Keith, on the other hand, spent several weeks of the summer in a closed room. His table was piled high with unmarked scripts to the left, marked ones to the right. Fair copies and lists of common errors, as well as what could be allowed and what could not, were pinned to the wall. For a month, we weren't allowed in that room, and when it was all over, Keith emerged vowing that never, never would he put himself through the ordeal again. Until the next year came round.

9

April in Paris

The *Worthing*, the *Brighton*, the *Arromanches*, the *Londres*, the *Lisieux* ... the five Newhaven-Dieppe ferries of the 1950s. We didn't much mind which one got us to and from France, so long as it wasn't the *Worthing*. It may have been state-of-the-art before the war and a hero of the Normandy landings, but now it was clapped out. It was withdrawn, only to re-appear, brightly painted and renamed, to spend its last years hauling cargo around the Greek islands.

On the morning of the first day of almost every Easter school holidays throughout the 1950s, we'd get ourselves from Steyning to Newhaven Harbour, cross to Dieppe, then take the boat-train on to Paris, the start of three weeks in Mitoune's *pension* in the least elegant part of fashionable Neuilly.

Of the five, we preferred the three French-owned ferries: the *Londres* was good, the *Arromanches* better, and the *Lisieux* newest and best. The moment you stepped aboard any of them you were in France – the language, the *matelots* in their jaunty uniforms, the smell of dark tobacco. And of course the food. Because, if the finances allowed, Keith would lead us to the ship's restaurant, where food was taken seriously and Paulette was in her element. Now she could do what people did in France, ask technical questions about the cuisine. If she tried that in England, she'd soon give up, seeing the shopkeeper's face and ours. But now, on French territory, she'd enter into dialogue with the waiter about the soup (which vegetables, how fresh?), the pork (Bayeux, Basque?), the steak (*filet, faux-filet, entrecote*?). We said nothing and looked the other way.

"Oh, you people," said Paulette, "you are so *English*."

At Dieppe, we walked down the gangplank as cargo and the occasional car were craned in huge nets from the ship's hold. Then we were on the platform looking up at the vast train of khaki carriages, searching for our reservations. Porters in blue smocks were pushing long-handled barrows called *diables*, devils. The air was a mixture of salt, tar and sulphurous smoke from the locomotive. Minutes later, its whistle shrieked as we began to crawl along the quayside, led by a man with a flag. We settled back in our compartment for the dash through the Normandy meadows and orchards, before we plunged in and out of the tunnels at Rouen, with the cathedral in a new position as we crossed the city. I liked to stand in the corridor to watch us overtake the convoys of barges on the Seine. After Pontoise, we started getting ready for arrival in Paris, and a little before six o'clock the Eiffel Tower came into view, and moments later the Sacré-Coeur. The brakes were applied as we passed Les Batignolles, and a minute later we were coming to a halt under the great roof of Gare Saint-Lazare.

If Lili was meeting us, we'd take a taxi to Neuilly. Otherwise it was the Métro, half an hour of tunnels which in those days were lined with an endlessly-repeated punning advert, *Dubo Dubon Dubonnet, Dubo Dubon Dubonnet*, one-two, one-two, one-two-three ... *Dubo* (*du beau*, some fine ...), *Dubon* (some good ...), *Dubonnet*, the aperitif. At our stop, Les Sablons, there was always a *mutilé de guerre*, a war invalid, begging. He might be playing an accordion or a mouth-organ. In the 1950s, such men were everywhere. Those who weren't playing an instrument or singing simply stood or sat in silence. They'd be holding out a tin, or there'd be a beret on the ground. After a few days, the shock wore off. But there was one I can't forget. He was standing with his head bowed and a cardboard sign around his neck. I don't recall what it said but I certainly remember that when I dropped a coin into his tin, it wasn't eyes that he raised in acknowledgement but two empty red sockets.

The *pension* in Neuilly was a handsome villa set back from the street in a courtyard near *la place du marché*, the open-air market where Mitoune bought all her supplies. She didn't own the *pension* but was running it on behalf of a Monsieur Marty. He

Mitoune. Toulouse. Circa 1944.

was gambling that with the help of Lili, who'd joined forces with her mother, the business would turn something of a profit. The omens, had he known, weren't good. Mitoune, Lili, Pitou all together under one roof had worked in Toulouse, but that was wartime, when everyone had to pull together. Now, the old tensions of the Aurillac days came back. And, as then, Pitou was the scapegoat.

Poor Pitou. He was kept firmly out of sight of the lodgers and particularly Lili. He stayed confined to the room he shared with Mitoune, and which I remember was permanently plunged in gloom. The shutters were never opened. Only in the quiet of the afternoon did Pitou dare emerge. I can see him still, opening the door bit by bit, peeping about from behind his bottle glasses, and when the coast was clear, shuffling to the kitchen to consume the food Mitoune left out for him. If you couldn't see him, you knew he was there by the slurping noises coming from the far side of the door. When he was done, he shuffled back to his room, and was gone for another twenty-four hours.

He relished the Easter visits of his grandchildren, Micou especially. He'd cast her as Cordelia to his King Lear. (Goneril and Regan were Paulette and Lili.) Every morning, Micou, Neil and I would take turns to enter his room. We'd kiss both his sandpapery cheeks, and find somewhere to perch on the double bed strewn with encyclopaedias, books, papers. He'd lay aside whatever he was reading and the magnifying glass he needed, and instantly a stream-of-consciousness monologue on history, geography, fishing, poetry, myth, mountains, music and, finally, the war. We knew that sooner or later he was sure to lead us back to Verdun.

Pitou did made some sorties, sometimes into Neuilly, occasionally into Paris, and once even to Steyning, with Mitoune. Paulette took snaps of them with her Kodak camera. Our grandparents are there sitting in the back yard at Southdown Terrace, he with a beret on his head and a walking-stick on his lap. Micou and Neil remember that visit for the rigmarole of the evening meal, the dual suppers. A harassed Paulette had to prepare two menus, an English one for us and something French for Mitoune and Pitou. Neil says the three of us would drift over to the French table to scrounge some of the much nicer dish our grandparents were enjoying.

My memory of that visit is the journey back to France with them. The weather was bad, and we crossed the Channel in a very heavy swell. Everyone was ill and lying on benches and on the floor. But Pitou sat bolt upright, quite unaffected, and told anyone who'd listen that the secret was to take a deep breath as the ship plunged down a trough, and let it out when the swell lifted us again.

We were wrong, I now see, to dine out on one particular sortie of Pitou's. He had to take some papers to the war pensions office in Bercy on the other side of Paris. Pitou planned the journey as if he'd been going to deepest Africa. The story is that he packed his old army kitbag with map, torch, compass, toothbrush, emergency rations, then shuffled to Les Sablons Métro station, descended and disappeared. A few hours later he returned, his kitbag unbroached. I'm ashamed we laughed at Pitou for this, because I think he was having an awful flashback of war. The Métro had become trenches, whose tunnels could collapse and bury him as different walls had buried comrades at Verdun.

Pitou's final sortie was to the army retirement home at Égletons, not far north of Aurillac. He made it soon after the death of Mitoune in July 1963, which came as the hugest of shocks. Only a few weeks earlier she'd been diagnosed with advanced lung and liver cancer. Her loss left Pitou inconsolable. It was no surprise that he lasted barely two more years in Égletons. In Steyning, Mitoune's death left us stunned and bereft. But Paulette felt something else as well: fury. She found herself weeping with rage one morning as she was cleaning the front-room fire. Her damned mother had done it again, put herself out of reach, only this time for ever. But part of Paulette's misery, I now think, was that she knew she'd been wrong to ignore the olive branch Mitoune had held out ten years earlier. It's only recently that I've come across the letter of contrition she wrote to Paulette in which she begs forgiveness for so many sins and errors. She's been a hopeless mother, she writes, and has failed her daughters. She feels worthless; she wants to die.

The letter didn't work. The anger that erupted that morning as Paulette knelt sweeping the grate would endure for years more, and even at the end of her life it seemed to me that while she's tried and tried to forgive her mother, in her heart she hadn't.

Front row, left to right: Jeanne, Mitoune, Pitou. Back row, left to right: Jacques, his wife Marcelle, Joseph husband of Jeanne. Bois de Boulogne, Paris. Circa 1961.

During our three weeks in Paris, we saw little of Keith. Every day he was off somewhere, busy with Educational Travel matters, arranging cultural programmes, sorting out venues, hostels, hotels, *lycées*. We saw a bit more of Paulette, but not that much, as we'd be shared out among the other adults. Paulette liked to go off on her own to the *Grands Magasins* to see what was in fashion. Once, I recall, she bought some cloth out of which a family friend who was an excellent amateur tailor made her a skirt and jacket. Sometimes she and Lili went off to the cinema. There was usually a good film showing at the Ranelagh in the 16th *arrondissement*. Or they might go with friends to a play at the Théâtre de L'Odéon in the 6th. We three children happily transferred our allegiance elsewhere. Mitoune loved to keep us with her. We'd accompany her to the marketplace, carry her shopping back, help her unpack it. We'd even offer to do some housework. And of course there were the audiences with Pitou. We spent time with Lili only really when Rolande – Rolande Rousse of the Toulouse years, now Madame Jean-Christophe Benoit – turned up with her husband and we all went out together, perhaps to the boating-lake in the Bois de Boulogne, perhaps to a cafe for pistachio ice-cream or a glass of luminous green *diabolo menthe*, sophistications as yet unknown in England. Rolande's husband, like her, was an operatic singer, a baritone; and they'd needed to move to the capital to further their careers. Hers was going slowly, the odd secondary role in Paris, better ones in the provinces. But his had taken off. Jean-Christophe quickly established himself both in light opera and as an interpreter of Ravel and Poulenc. Until a near-fatal injury in his mid-70s injured his brain, he was a cheery extrovert and a natural showman, gathering audiences as he quipped, punned and told risqué jokes. He cut a bit of a dash, but was too short and square for the suits he liked to wear. They made him look like a dance-band leader. But when he opened his mouth it was a different matter. He'd arrive at the *pension*, bound up the steps, whack open the front door, and his *"Bonjour tout le monde!"* would ring down the hallway like the opening scene of an operetta.

What we children liked best was to be taken in their car to where they lived. First they had a black Citroën Traction Avant, as seen in gangster films, and then one of the first space-age DS saloons. We'd ride as if on air along avenue de la Grande Armée, circle the Arc de Triomphe, cruise down the Champs-Elysées to Place de la Concorde, the Tuileries, the Louvre, the Bastille, and at Place de la Nation, we'd turn left up boulevard Voltaire to Place de la République and soon we'd be outside the Benoit's apartment in rue Ramey in higgledy-pig-gledy Montmartre, not far below the Sacré-Coeur. We'd buy baguettes and Rolande would make us all *tartines au beurre*, the baguettes halved lengthwise and spread thick with more delicacies we knew nothing of in England yet, butter that was unsalted and *confiture aux myrtilles*, bilberry jam.

But it was best to discover Paris on your own, I decided, and from our third visit, when I'd turned fourteen, I was allowed to do just that. I took buses and the Métro to places that sounded interesting: Place des Vosges, Canal Saint-Martin, Ile Saint-Louis, Vincennes. But mostly I was drawn to the Latin Quarter. I'd sit in the Luxembourg Garden and pretend to read a book when really I was studying the students on their way to the Sorbonne, trying to ape their nonchalance. On other days I'd take the old bus that did the no. 43 route. I'd pick it up at the stop two minutes away from the *pension*, and adopt a position on the outside platform at the rear. I'd inhale the dark aroma of the cigarettes passengers were allowed to smoke on the platform. We made our way along avenue du Roule, avenue des Ternes, then onto tree-lined boulevard Haussmann and past the apartment where Marcel Proust, of whom I'd only recently heard, spent years writing his masterpiece. Whenever the bus stopped I made it my business – as casually as I could – to unfasten and refasten the chain to let people hop on and off. I might go on to the terminus at Gare du Nord, or alight earlier at Saint-Augustin and make for the music section of the various *Grands Magasins* to seek out records by Georges Brassens. As everyone in the family (except Keith) adored Brassens, I'd have been given the money to buy his latest EP, those small extended play records that had a wide hole in the middle requiring an adaptor for our English turntable. Brassens sang gentle-sounding songs that in reality were punchy satires of the Church, the Army, the Government, transgression, foibles and folly. But he could be warm and uncomplicated too. His tender ballad in honour of the person who fed and sheltered him when he was down on his luck might not have been his greatest song, but for us it was particularly resonant as that person was an Auvergnat.

And too soon our three weeks were up. The start of the school summer term was imminent. Back in England, we tried to pretend we'd never left Paris. We spoke only French. We went on with *petits déjeuners* of *café au lait, biscottes, confiture aux myrtilles*. We played our Brassens records. I went where I couldn't be found to smoke the Gauloises I'd sneaked home in my luggage.

None of it, the speaking French, the breakfasts, the Brassens, lasted more than a week. The Gauloises defeated me and I distributed the rest of the packet at school. Paris was over for another year.

10

110 Not Out

It's a bright Saturday morning, the first one of the school summer term. We've been back from Paris no more than three days. The aroma coming down the stairs is of linseed oil. On the top landing, a leather bag, a sort of oblong Gladstone, has been fetched from the cupboard where it's spent the winter. The whitened boots have been placed at the bottom, then the jockstrap with the box, the genital protector that looks like a codpiece. The cream cable-knit sweater has followed, then the cream flannels, the white shirt and socks. The cap, striped light blue and yellow, has been squeezed into a corner, the gloves tucked inside it, and the two white leg-pads fitted over the lot. The remaining space is for the long-handled wooden bat, its face a flat surface, the reverse keel-shaped. It gleams with recent oil, lustrous as good furniture, and it's that that's the source of the aroma. Over the banister has been draped the blazer, the same blue and yellow stripes as the cap, and with a heraldic shield sewn onto the breast pocket. Before sitting down to lunch, Keith fetches the bag down; this afternoon he's playing cricket.

For most seasons of the thirteen years we lived in Steyning, Keith was a regular in the cricket club's first XI. The club took itself seriously, and was remarkably strong for a small town. Its best player during Keith's time, Trevor Adcock, had played for one of the Sussex County sides. The Steyning club allowed him to wear his Sussex cap. There were other fine players, among whom Keith was prominent. As an undergraduate, he'd played for London University and had captained some of its teams. (Not just cricket, football too.) In 1935 or 1936, a scout from Middlesex Cricket Club watched him, and was sufficiently impressed to offer him a trial. Nothing came of it, possibly because Middlesex lost interest, possibly because Keith did, which is just as likely as Keith can't have fancied earning a livelihood scoring a few runs and then standing for hours in the out field at Chelmsford or Northampton or Cardiff. I doubt he'd have joined in the card games in the pavilion when rain stopped play, or sunk pints of beer in the station buffet, waiting for the last train home.

It's a well-worn cliché that for many Englishmen cricket is a religion. For a while our family tried to get the faith. We'd go to many of Keith's matches. The fixtures alternated, one Saturday at home, on Steyning's ground below the Round Hill. The next Saturday, the game would be in, say, Cowfold, Partridge Green, Pease Pottage. Often the whole family went, even Paulette, who understood nothing of the rules and didn't want to, but liked seeing the players turned out so elegantly all in white. I went to the matches more consistently than anyone else. I'd walk along with my father, each of us carrying our bag, mine a smaller one containing a half-size bat, a set of plastic stumps, and a lightweight plastic ball. Before the match got under way, I'd look for anyone prepared to give me a game of French cricket. But as soon as there was action on the field, I packed my bag and went over to a white hut where I attached myself to gentle, pipe-smoking old Mr Hurst, who sat inside it keeping a ball-by-ball record of the game in the club's large scorebook. He and the team captain always arrived early for home games. They'd give the pitch an inspection, pacing up and down, testing its firmness with their feet, squatting to give it a few prods with a penknife. Once satisfied, the captain returned to the pavilion, and Mr Hurst continued to his hut. There he fetched out the wooden boxes which contained square slates, each marked with a numeral, and which would be hung to a board so that everyone watching (except Paulette) could follow the score. Watching and listening to Mr Hurst and the visiting team's scorer alongside him, I learnt the special language of cricket. What didn't register with me, though, until later was how much that language echoed the warfare which several of the players on the pitch would have been involved in a few years earlier. Nor did I realise that among the spectators were survivors of an earlier war, the one that I'd heard so much about from Pitou. All sport uses the language of war, of course; but cricket's seems particularly apt for what these two generations of men must have known. Balls *rained down* like shells but the batsmen *stood their ground*; they *dug in* for a long *war of attrition*; a batsman might be the *casualty* of a ball that had zoomed like a *grenade*; he'd gone *cheaply*; wickets *fell* steadily until there was just *the last man standing*.

One summer, I left Mr Hurst and his hut because I and Robin, my Saturday-afternoon friend, had decided to have our own scorebooks. We bought ourselves a junior version each, reduced size and paper-bound. We stocked up on Venus 2H pencils, two erasers and one penknife to share. I wish my book had survived. I wish too that we still had the cuttings from the local newspapers reporting the legendary innings Keith played one afternoon. I remember the headlines – 110 NOT OUT! – and the accounts of his magnificent *knock*. We have no record of it, nor even the memory, as it occurred on one of the few Saturdays when for some reason no one in the family went to watch the game. But I can imagine how Keith constructed his innings. There'd have been the correct stance, left shoulder forward, the careful footwork, the back-lift and follow-through of the bat, the forward and backward defensives strokes shielding his stumps, the late cuts executed with finesse, the square cuts perfectly timed, the off drives slammed, the cover drives clouted, the singles and twos nudged and chipped, even the odd three risked. Only when the right delivery came would Keith have threaded the ball through the tightest of gaps straight along the ground to the boundary for a four. There wouldn't have been any sixes; those were for the Flash Harrys. Keith would have given the fielders few chances, possibly none at all as he remained *not out*, he *carried his bat*, outlasting every one of his ten teammates. At the end, he'd have walked back to the pavilion amidst the applause from the opposing team and pats on the back from his own side. Spectators would have risen from their benches and deck chairs to salute him. But Keith would have shrugged off the fuss, and hurried into the dressing-room to remove his pads and gloves and the box from inside his jockstrap. He'd have emerged to get himself a cup of tea and plot the remainder of the match with his teammates. In the evening, unwilling hero, he'd have been marched into the Norfolk Arms but declined the beers offered him.

Members of all generations of the family have a copy of a professional photo of Keith taken in the early years of his cricketing career, not on the day of the "110 Not Out". Keith and his fellow-batsman are walking out to the crease to open the innings. Keith is wearing the kit I recognise from his Gladstone bag. The other batsman is a little shorter. The whiteness of their clothes deepens their complexions. Keith has that English air, reserved but stylish, that so beguiled Mitoune and even, I think, Lili. He could have been cast in one of the black-and-white war films we went to see in Brighton. He'd not have been out of place on the bridge of a Royal Navy frigate. We didn't tell him, of course; it didn't do to speak of one's looks. Or the war.

Around my fourteenth birthday, Keith decided to teach me how to play cricket. He got me to pick up his bat, but, because I was small for my age and the bat was full sized, I had to place my hands too low down the handle. Keith shifted them up; I

Keith, right, and partner opening the batting. Circa 1938.

lowered them. We found a compromise. Then Keith gripped each of my calves in turn and set my legs in the right stance to protect my wicket and give the bowler nothing to aim at. He guided my back-lift, nudged my shoulders to the proper angle and adjusted my elbows. Then, his hands on the handle as well as mine, we steered the blade upwards together, held it, and brought it down onto the imaginary ball. But I couldn't get the hang of it. So Keith changed tack. Since I was left-handed, I should forget about batting and try spin-bowling. I did, and to my surprise became reasonable enough to earn a place in the school's Second XI.

But my heart wasn't in cricket, and three seasons later I abandoned it once and for all. I'd discovered another sport, which came more naturally to me. For a long time I'd had a friend called Andy Treacher whose family lived in a large Edwardian villa with its own lawn-tennis court. Andy and I decided one summer to put it to good use. Though he was the more skilful of us, I thought I got pretty good, and I wanted my parents to see me play. Paulette obliged, but not Keith. Tennis, he said, like all racquet sports was for cissies.

I'm sure my father would find little to enjoy about cricket today. He'd be disgusted by the sponsorship, the logos, the brash limited-over games and day-and-night matches, the flashy clothing and the baseball caps. He'd be appalled by the sledging, and dismayed at the scandals and corruption. His were the dying days of the Corinthian, the gentleman amateur. If he were here now, though, I'd try again to persuade him of the virtues of tennis if only because Wimbledon remains the one sporting event I can think of in which players not only must wear white but behave with the courtesy (if you ignore the grunting) that's gone for good from cricket.

11

End of Term

Two moments that occurred at roughly the same time signalled the end of childhood for me: the afternoon I saw the film *Rock Around the Clock*; and the evening I witnessed the first of my parents' many rows.

I'd been channelling my energies into schoolwork, sports and locospotting, that national craze among boys for collecting engine numbers. It was a hobby much less mocked then than now. For one thing, in the post-war era of austerity there were few pastimes so cheap. It cost just one penny to buy the platform ticket which let you sit all day on a station and watch the action. All you needed was a notebook, a pencil and the sandwiches your mum made for you. If you misbehaved, a porter could clip your ear without risk of prosecution. And if you couldn't afford the penny, you could stand on a bridge or sit in a field by the track. There was more to it than writing down numbers. I'd save up months of pocket money to go on expeditions that needed hours of careful plotting. I'd match timetables to maps and learnt a lot about geography and logistics. In the holidays, there'd be pre-dawn departures with friends on the workmen's train to London, ten hours going round the termini, and home on the last departure from Victoria. Our parents were happy to let us do it. In those days, it was thought safe to let children roam alone. So no one opposed the most ambitious of my odysseys, Steyning to Exeter and back in a day, three changes of train in one direction and three in the reverse. It was thanks to the names of the engines on that route that I first heard of King Arthur and his knights called Sir Bors de Ganis, Sir Mador de la Porte, Sir Dodinas le Savage, Sir Cador of Cornwall, and some more. And the further I roamed, the more towns of southern England I discovered: Tunbridge Wells and Bexhill to the east, Southampton and Salisbury to the west, Reading to the north. I learnt from a book about railway photography, and tried my hand with Paulette's little Kodak. And using the kit I'd been given by a family friend, I made stabs at developing and printing what I'd taken.

I think Keith saw that my pursuits should be indulged, that in a roundabout way they were helping me grow up. They'd need soon to give way to more mature interests, of course, but meanwhile he'd play along. So, when we were together on a train, he'd make a point of calling out engine numbers for me to write down. Then he decided it was time I had a more gracious experience of the railways than engine-depots and platform ends. We'd have a day out in London, he announced, travelling on the luxurious Brighton Belle. On the day, we settled into our woven-tapestry chairs and as the Belle pulled out of the station, I remember, my father and I laughed together on finding the menu boasted Baked Beans upon Toast. *Upon*!

The Brighton Belle stayed in my memory, but only for so long. It and railways were forgotten the day the music of Bill Hayley and the Comets hit me in the solar plexus. By chance I heard his record "Rock Around the Clock" one night on the wireless. Where on earth did music like this come from? I discovered there was a companion film, same name, same music, same musicians, and that it was coming to the Regent in Brighton, where I saw it twice through. I emerged knowing that a very different phase of my life had begun, and as much as possible I'd spend it in Brighton, seedy, steamy Brighton, the proving-ground of my adolescence.

And then there was that first row I witnessed between my parents. I dare say I knew there were fault-lines in their marriage, but not how much they widened. Keith was wretched. I didn't know why, but what we all saw was that he was becoming withdrawn. And the more he withdrew, the more Paulette went after him. I must have caught one of the moments, that evening, when he was cornered, and it wasn't pretty. Nor was the next . . . or the next . . .

I wondered if I might do something to bring my parents together. So I listened to the rows from a safe distance and wait for the opening which allowed me in. I found Paulette, who was only too willing to explain herself to me. I can't recall too well what she said, though the odd remark has stuck: "your father needs a housemaid, not a wife", or "he doesn't need a wife at all, he's wedded to that school". I ran to find Keith, rephrasing Paulette's argument in my head. Keith would say a few words, none of which I can remember. And back I'd go, the shuttle diplomat. I thought I was sorting things out, but I was wrong. A truce occurred only when and because the combatants were exhausted. I'd made no difference. But I did learn one valuable lesson which would serve me well a decade later, when I realised that I'd make an awful social worker, and swiftly gave up the training course.

Keith and his problems remained a closed book to me. But I did begin to understand where Paulette's distress came from: loneliness. Her sense of isolation was at its most acute in the Steyning years of the 1950s – Britain's most class-conscious decade, as it happens. There was a lot going against Paulette: one, she was a foreigner; two, a French one at that; three, she'd married into a profession of little esteem; four, she went out to work. She'd already had a taste of English attitudes at Lytchett Manor School fifteen years before. But in Bradford and Hounslow, in the war that followed, her class and the fact that she was foreign hadn't mattered. She'd been accepted for the person she was. But in Steyning, she lived on the defensive, not knowing how to behave. One day, she'd be more English than the English: dullest clothes, French accent disguised as much as possible, all smiles, nods and agreement. The next day, she'd exaggerate her Frenchness: the chic clothes from Paris, the stronger accent, the deliberate confrontations. One thing she could never do was to emulate our market-gardener neighbour. Mr Radzinski had decided to keep his head down, say little to anyone, speak only Polish, as if he'd never left his country. Paulette was too gregarious and full of natural curiosity for that. She was on reasonable terms with a small number of Steyning people, but it was two other foreigners that I think she gravitated most frequently: Konrad Rodan, an urbane Czech pathologist who always wore bow ties; and Raoul Casares, a debonair oil executive of Argentinian extraction. These were Paulette's allies. Yet to me they seemed more at ease in Steyning than did Paulette. That, I think, was because they each held two cards that Paulette didn't: their professions were highly regarded; and they were men.

Paulette's distress steadily got worse, so it shouldn't have come as a surprise to hear there might be another man in her life. But it did. I decided that it must be someone she'd met through her teaching and examining. Or maybe a Frenchman in Paris. It turned out, improbably, to be an auctioneer at the Steyning livestock market, a large and heavy man, tow-haired and ruddy-complexioned, who went about dressed in the uniform of his trade: brogues, cavalry twills, houndstooth jacket, flat cap. All we'd heard about him was a story that he'd rigged the bidding for a magnificent turkey Paulette had her eye on and that he knew she couldn't afford. Something like this:

"Start me at two pounds, somebody."

Silence.

"Thirty shillings."

Nothing.

"One pound."

Still nothing.

Then Paulette plunges:

"Ten shillings!"

And before other bidders can react, bang, down comes the gavel.

"Sold to Mrs Sorrell for ten shillings!"

The figures are guesswork. So is the story of Paulette's romance, if that's ever what it was. She didn't abandon us, nor do I remember any more talk about the auctioneer. She tried to form a bond with a family of German Jews traumatised by the concentration camps, but they were too haunted to get close to her. There was Ivy Treacher, mother of my friend Andy, and Margaret Rodan, wife of the Czech pathologist, and other friendships which did something to lessen the loneliness.

And then Vera Joynes arrived. Vera was returning to England from Canada with her two sons following her divorce. In the mid-1950s, divorce was still a dirty word. Vera was unfussed by public opinion, an attitude Paulette greatly envied. Vera's mind was focused on other things, one in particular: spiritualism. She'd met a medium called Vi, and was attending her séances. Vi had a remarkable gift for healing. Through her spirit-guide – she called him Silver Star – she made accurate diagnoses of what it was that afflicted the people who came to her or those who sent her possessions for her to "read". Vera's elder son, my friend Andrew, told me recently that he himself went to see Vi for a "reading". After the introductions, the session began. Light-voiced and physically small, Vi became transformed. She seemed to take on volume and grow twice her size; and when she spoke, the voice was that of a man, presumably Silver Star. Had Andrew told me the story at the time, I'd not have wanted to believe him. The spiritualism in which so many bereaved people had placed their faith in the First World War had passed out of fashion in the scientific New Elizabethan age. So when Vera came evangelising, as often she did, I shut my ears. She had more success with Paulette. She even took her to meet Vi

121

and possibly to attend a séance. What *is* certain, because a letter about it has survived, is that Paulette asked Vi to help Lili. Whatever her problem – the letter doesn't say – Lili wasn't getting far with her doctors in Paris. She was persuaded to send Vi a clean handkerchief for her to read. Vi had not been told a thing about the handkerchief's owner, but her diagnosis contained so many home truths that Lili resolved to mend her ways. Whether she tried is another matter. My aunt was one of life's determined sceptics.

*

At about the time Harold McMillan was telling the country that we'd never had it so good, Keith was deciding that he'd never had it so bad at Steyning Grammar School. That apparently was the cause of the unhappiness I couldn't fathom. The problem was the headmaster, we were told. The man was running a successful and, to my mind, happy school. I felt settled there, and Neil too for the time he stayed before he transferred to a school which would teach him music. The odd criminal aside, the headmaster had assembled a talented, conscientious and trustworthy staff. Academically, our small school was punching way above its weight. It got an absurdly high proportion of its pupils into university. But obviously something I couldn't see was frustrating Keith and had made him so restless that he decided he must leave not only this school but give up teaching altogether. Educational Travel Ltd – the company that facilitated our family trips not only to France, but also to Switzerland, Italy and Spain – offered him a salaried position. First he satisfied himself it would be permanent, secure and pensionable, then tendered his resignation from the Grammar School. Although he'd be out of teaching, as he wanted, he'd still be in the world of education, as he also wanted. His base would be at the company office in Norwood, but he'd spend most of his time visiting schools up and down the United Kingdom and abroad to promote the internationalist cause and Educational Travel's programme of holiday courses, cultural visits and exchanges. We'd be moving to Horsham, chosen because nowhere was better placed. The agreement was that Educational Travel would buy a house which we'd rent from them at a modest cost. One was found in the centre of the town, convenient for the station where Keith would catch a fast train to Norwood, Paulette a direct one to Pulborough, and Neil and I our slow one to Steyning. Micou would have the best deal, just a ten-minute walk to her school.

In the assembly at the end of the autumn term of 1959, the school sang Hymn 333 Part II, "Lord dismiss us with thy blessing", and Keith said a few words of farewell.

We had our last Christmas in Southdown Terrace, and on the morning of Thursday 31st December, in the final hours of the 1950s, we said goodbye to Steyning, some of us with heavier hearts than Paulette's.

*

It's a bright day in mid-August 2016, and Claire and I are having a sandwich on the cricket ground in Steyning where Keith made his celebrated 110 Not Out. I'd have liked us to arrive by train on our old branch-line down from Horsham or up from Shoreham, but that's not been possible for half a century. Dr Beeching killed it off in 1966, on my birthday, what's more. So we've driven in the A283, past what the great storm of 1987 has left of Chanctonbury Ring, and then along the bypass that's been built on the old railway track-bed.

We finish our sandwich and set off for King's Stone Avenue, down the long straight to Bramber Castle, and then left past where Tom Carr's shack stood, a visionary who strode through the fields dressed like a mediaeval halberdier, shouting at the clouds. We reach King's Stone Avenue and at the far end, no. 25. It comes as a nice surprise that in six decades the house has hardly changed. The façade is the same apart from the glossy paintwork and the windows, now double-glazed. It still looks like an extra large dolls' house. I stand in the road and point my camera. Someone in no. 23 has spotted me. He comes out. I assure him I'm not a stalker, I'm not planning a burglary, but I lived next door once upon a time. Mr 23 relaxes. He tells us that Gillian, the owner of no. 25, would have loved to show us round, but she's out at work. He offers us a tour of his house instead. The hall and front room are smaller than I remember, but not as dark. The new picture windows let in much more light, which gets reflected by the sanded floorboards. The kitchen is about four times the size of the cubby-hole where Paulette did her cooking. No. 23's has grown outwards into the back garden. We're taken out into it, which like those of the other houses is long and narrow. The rear elevations of the whole row have changed. The dormers that have been added make the houses look alarmingly top-heavy, as if they're about to overbalance.

We take our leave and head up King's Barn Lane. We cross the bridge where the lorry fractured my skull when I was eight, and reach Southdown Terrace. I think of parking there but decide not to risk the car's tyres. In sixty years, the Council has done nothing to improve the road. So we park near the church and walk back. The terrace is an anticlimax, no less faded than when we lived there. I'm disappointed. These handsome Victorian houses should stand nobly, but they seem to be slouching. It might have been better to pull it down when the railway and the cattle market over the road, and the Railway Hotel, and Mr Radzinski's smallholding at the rear, all disappeared. The terrace seems dead. There's not a soul about, so we don't linger. We return to the car and start westward.

A few miles from Steyning, we stop at a cafe. Our morale needs a lift. We order a pot of tea and two rock buns, which are every bit as delicious as they look. We take our time. Then, restored and cheered up, we compliment our waitress as we pay the bill. She tells us it was her husband made the rock buns. Her accent is heavy. We ask her where she's from. Romania, they both are. So, I have to ask, where does she think Brexit will leave them?

"We don't know," she says. "We've lived in UK for many years, we work hard, we don't claim benefits, we pay our taxes. I think we are OK but my husband not so much. He asks why your country doesn't like us."

We continue westwards. Claire is driving. I close my eyes and think about that Romanian couple. Then my thoughts turn to Keith and Paulette. They'd both be exactly one hundred years old now. I'm thankful they didn't live to experience Brexit. Too many hopes snuffed out with the candles on the cake.

12

Black Box

We'd been in the Horsham house – which, incidentally, Paulette loathed, a neat box on the outside, a hopelessly-planned refrigerator within – no more than a couple of months before Keith realised that his change of job had been a catastrophic error. Far from roving ambassador, he was a desk-bound pen-pushing commuter whose task was to answer the phone, process forms and lick envelopes. He struggled on for a few more weeks. He'd be out of the house before seven am and not back until after seven pm, Monday to Friday. At the weekend, he was fit for nothing. He began to rise late, drift through Saturday and Sunday, and go to bed early. We realised just how bad things were the day Neil came across him slumped in an armchair, weeping. At some point – perhaps April or May – he stopped altogether going to his office and took to his bedroom. He re-appeared only to pick at some food or visit the doctor. If he was prescribed medication, it did nothing. I'm sure he wasn't having any talking therapy either.

It was now a crisis, which Paulette rose to with a grace and determination which make me think of Grand'mère in Jussac and Mitoune in Aurillac. Three generations of women needing to be stronger than their men. Paulette was composed and organised. She made sure nothing interfered with the lives of us three children, all at important stages of our education. She ran the house, took over Keith's desk, paying bills, writing letters, making appointments. And all the while she travelled to and from her school twenty-five miles away. I assume Educational Travel went on paying Keith's salary, but maybe not, and we became wholly reliant on Paulette's earnings, in effect, a single-parent family.

From left to right: Neil, Micou, Paulette, Martin. Horsham. January 1961.

"It was a very black period," Paulette said. "I began to wonder if your father would ever work again. I was terrified Educational Travel would turf us out of the house. I couldn't sleep. I stayed up at night writing out plans for our future. We were really short of money. I began to think that the only solution was for you to give up the idea of university, Martin, and find a job in Horsham."

We saw that Keith had had a big setback but couldn't understand why it became a total collapse. It didn't matter surely that his new job hadn't worked out. He'd walk straight back into teaching. There were plenty of schools locally: Collyer's, the boys' grammar school, and Christ's Hospital and Cranleigh, nearby public schools. Educational Travel would let us stay on in the house, at least for a while.

But Keith wasn't registering a thing, his depression was so bad. I remember Paulette's suggesting that the trauma of his parents' death and his refusal to fight in the war were the real reasons. I could understand about his parents, but not the pacifism. He hadn't been an appeaser, as I saw it (and still do). He'd stood up with courage and resolution for a deep principle, and he'd accepted the consequences. He should have been proud of himself. He didn't know, any more than anyone else, about the Nazi death camps. If he had, he might well have thought again. No, said Paulette much later. She suspected from the start – but wasn't sure, and Keith would never open up – that the shame he felt came from something else, that his refusal had not been so much to fight as to take orders. He was damned if he'd do what some fool in a uniform told him to. And that, Paulette added, was the problem at Steyning Grammar School. The headmaster was too authoritarian for Keith. Depression, one theory has it, is the depressed person's aggression turned back on itself. In Keith's case, I think that makes sense, though he did direct rage outwards when he whacked a cricket ball or a miscreant's backside, as Neil once found out.

The weeks ground on. Keith got steadily worse. It was decided he must be admitted to a mental hospital, and at the end of the summer of 1960, that's what happened.

It's January 2017. I've crossed the parkland on the north side of the Chichester Festival Theatre and glimpsed what must be the old water-tower of Graylingwell Hospital, where Keith was brought fifty-seven years ago. I'm on my way to the university, which happens to be next door, where I'm meeting the historian Hugo Frey. No one knows more about Graylingwell, the West Sussex County Asylum as it was first called.

I find Hugo outside his office, and we walk the short distance up to Graylingwell Park, the residential complex the hospital became after its closure in 2009. I'm struck by the size of the site. The fact is, says Hugo, that the hospital's catchment area was very wide. Over its 104 years of existence, it treated an enormous number of patients. In 1956, for example, its population was as high as 1150. Hugo steers me past luxury apartments that once were the female wing, and then the treatment rooms, the male wing, the dormitories, refectories, storesheds, workshops, boiler-houses, the day-rooms, the plumbers' and carpenters' shops, offices, pump-house and the chapel. By 2021, there will be a total of eight hundred homes, plus community centres, enterprise studios, a creative hub and a youth club. I must say that what has already been achieved looks most attractive. This, we joke, is one madhouse we'd be delighted to live in.

As we walk round, I try to identify the block where Paulette brought me to see Keith one miserable afternoon, but I can't. The memory is too faint. Hugo says I'll find out more from Katherine Slay at the County Record Office. I make my way there and explain my aim to Katherine. She can let me see some but not all the files I'd like. Some are restricted under the Data Protection Act. Nevertheless, I learn new things. Keith was sent to Graylingwell on 2nd September 1960, and stayed for less time than I'd always believed, four weeks to the day. After that, I'd also assumed, he was discharged and came home. But then I read that on 30th September he was transferred to the Royal West Sussex Hospital on Broyle Road, half a mile away. This is as far as I get. Katherine says I won't find the reason for Keith's transfer nor how long he remained in the Royal West Sussex because that hospital also has closed and the records I need have been destroyed. It's very frustrating. I wanted records of my father's treatment. And as we know that at some point he contracted jaundice, I'd have liked to know if that was the reason for his transfer to the Royal West Sussex. Or had he contracted it before even he went to Graylingwell, let alone the RWS? That's exactly what Keith maintained later. He was adamant that his problem all along had been jaundice. He conceded that he might have had a touch of depression, but that was because, as everyone knew, jaundice caused depression, and not the other way round.

I find out from the Graylingwell reports that the Mental Health Act of 1959, the year before Keith was admitted, had been a significant attempt to improve the public perception of mental illness and to enhance patients' rights. Some of the language changed. The word "asylum" was dropped and was replaced by Mental Hospital; and patients no longer would be categorised as Voluntary, Temporary or Certified, but as Informal, Observation or Treatment. Keith's status, I read, was Informal, the erstwhile Voluntary. This comes as a surprise as I'd thought he'd been taken to Graylingwell against his will. I find out that he was housed in Summersdale, the reception ward, where he remained for all of his four weeks. These details combine to make me almost certain that he came in under Section 25 of the 1959 Act, which reads: "Section 25 patients come for observation for a period not exceeding 28 days. Application for admission is made either by the nearest relative or by a Mental Welfare Officer supported by two medical recommendations." My guess would be that three people

applied to have Keith taken into Graylingwell: Paulette, Keith's
GP and Konrad Rodan, their pathologist friend.

During his month in Summersdale Keith underwent one
session of electroconvulsive therapy (ECT), and maybe more.
He was to remain angry about it forever afterwards, convinced
he hadn't needed it and that it hadn't done him any good.
Because it was, and to an extent remains, a controversial tech-
nique, I want to find out how it was done. How many sessions
did Keith have? What exactly was the procedure? Was it as
grim as the infamous scene in *One Flew Over the Cuckoo's Nest*?
Did Keith see the same blue light crackling through the air that
Sylvia Plath describes in *The Bell Jar*? I've read that the way
of administering ECT was modified around 1960. I hope that
Keith's treatment came after the change was made as henceforth patients received a general anaesthetic. A mercy, because
without it some had convulsions so violent that bones got broken, large as well as small. With luck, then, Keith was out of
it while the electric current was passed through his brain. I
read in the 1960 report that the Graylingwell protocol com-
bined ECT with Imipramine and monoamine oxidase inhibi-
tors (new drugs at the time, the latter an improbable derivative
of rocket fuel abandoned by the Nazis). It was thought this
combination helped reduce the rate of relapse after recovery.
Drugs or no drugs, ECT has always sounded an alarming and
drastic procedure to me, and I suspect that Keith had no right
to refuse it. As a voluntary patient, his consent was not a legal
requirement.

I know some of the literary accounts of depression: Robert
Burton, Dante, William Styron and Hamlet's speech on the
subject ("I have of late – wherefore I know not – lost all my
mirth ..."). Recently I read Andrew Solomon's magisterial *The
Noonday Demon*. I was looking for an account of how ECT is
administered. Solomon's is the most detailed I've seen. Blood
tests are followed by a chest X-ray and a check on the patient's

tolerance of anaesthetics. The patient signs a consent form and, the night before treatment, receives food intravenously. In the morning, he or she is wired up to monitors, gel is rubbed onto the temples and electrodes are applied. The treatment will be either unilateral, to the non-dominant side of the brain, or bilateral. Unilateral shocks have fewer side effects than bilateral, and can be equally effective. After the general anaesthetic – effective for about ten minutes – and a muscle relaxant, the patient is connected to both an EEG and an ECG machine which simultaneously monitor the brain and the heart. Then a shock of one second's duration is given, causing a seizure that lasts for about half a minute. The electrical output is equivalent to that of a 100-Watt bulb. Though most of the charge is absorbed by soft tissue and the skull, it's powerful enough to alter the chemistry of the brain. Within a quarter of an hour, the patient wakes up in the recovery room.

No one seems to know why ECT should work, but it does, and now, 2017, it's still in favour. It doesn't work for everyone, however, and there are plenty of patients who, like Keith, remain convinced that they hadn't needed it. Keith would not be shifted from his conviction that his problem had been purely physical. The stress of a job he shouldn't have been doing had worn him down, lowered his resistance, hence the jaundice. Nothing more, nothing less. But something had changed him for the better. I was amazed. He was no longer the zombie slumped on a garden bench that I'd seen on my one visit to Graylingwell. He had a good colour again and he walked with a firm stride. He didn't go back to his job with Educational Travel, but continued his association with them. To his relief and Paulette's, there was no talk yet of their repossessing the house.

He was eager to get back into teaching. He'd realised that he should never have left the classroom. If ever there was a born teacher, Keith was it. Now, though, he feared it would prove as difficult as in the 1940s to find a position. Not because of his pacifism this time, but the stigma of mental illness. I don't know how many jobs he'd applied for by the time Hazelwick School, one of the new comprehensives in Crawley, offered him a post. It wasn't ideal, only part-time and certainly not his kind of school. But he was back in the right profession. It turned out to be a double blessing, in fact. It resolved a separate problem, where to live. Sooner or later, Educational Travel would want to sell our house, not to us, as it would be beyond our means. As it happens, they let us stay on in Springfield Crescent five more years. Two things make me think our financial worries had begun to ease. One: I wasn't sent out to work, but went away to university instead. Two: we acquired a cleaning-lady, the wonderful and wonderfully-named Mrs Northeast, Madame Nord-Est as she was known in Neuilly. My guess is that Paulette had increased her hours at St Michael's School to earn the money to buy the help that let her spend more time at St Michael's earning the money to buy the help.

Micou entered the Sixth Form at her High School. Neil had already started at Ifield Grammar in Crawley, to which Keith would soon transfer from Hazelwick and where he became what he'd been in Steyning, schoolmaster to one of his own children. Neil had had to leave Steyning since music wasn't on the syllabus, and music was where his future lay. At Ifield, he was taught by some outstanding musicians, and he brought home the results. We got to hear composers new to us, and discovered works by others already familiar. In our last summer, Neil introduced us to a work we knew only by name. For the inauguration of the gramophone he'd been saving for – a Pye Black Box – we gathered to listen to Bach's Forty-Eight Preludes and Fugues for keyboard. The French windows were open to the warmth of the evening sun. I thought, now that Keith was restored, how symbolic it seemed that Bach's keyboard should be described as well-tempered.

13

The Battle for Hastings

When the time approached to vacate the house in Horsham, Keith and Paulette set about the long and difficult search for somewhere they could afford. Eventually they found it, not in Horsham but in the last place they wanted to be: Crawley New Town.

What made it financially viable was the fact that Keith was employed by one of its schools. Generous mortgage deals were on offer to people who worked or were prepared to work in the town. Keith and Paulette decided to buy, off-plan, a three-bedroom semi in the Furnace Green district, close to Tilgate Forest. Micou thinks it cost around £4,000. They'd now have a foot on the ladder, and would find somewhere nicer soon. Once no. 7 Fontwell Road was ready, Keith and Paulette moved in ... and stayed for twenty years without, so they claimed, getting to know a soul apart from their GP and some shopkeepers. I can almost believe it. In term time, they were too caught up in their work to think of much else. Paulette spent most weekdays at St Michael's. Keith had more chance to involve himself in the life of Crawley, but he'd decided at the outset that the place was awful and he'd have as little as possible to do with it. They had a daily routine which hardly varied down the years. They'd be up at dawn, and at around seven Keith would drive Paulette to Crawley station in the Ford Popular they were buying "on the never never". Keith went on to Ifield Grammar, and when school was over for the day, the journeys would be made in reverse. Back in the house, they'd light a fire or sit in the garden, depending on the season, have some supper, mark some homework, watch some television and go to bed.

In time, Keith renewed his association with Educational Travel, on the same unpaid and part-time basis as before his breakdown. The work he now did for them, the same kind as before his breakdown, occupied much of the school holidays and got him away from Crawley. In 1970, the first of the Easter French language and culture courses he devised took place in Versailles, a stone's throw from Louis XIV's great palace. The course was designed for British sixth-formers. Keith enlisted the backing of the French cultural services, which recruited a dozen young teachers from the Paris lycées. Paulette had a major role as liaison officer and unofficial chaperone to the girls on the course, most of whom were travelling abroad for the first time. Year by year the course grew in size and

Closing vin d'honneur. Versailles Easter Course. Circa 1971.

PAULETTE

success, and by the time it ceased functioning (I think in the late 1970s), it had become the linchpin of Educational Travel's programme and Keith's greatest contribution to the company. The Versailles courses were a personal triumph for him. I know, because I was there for some of them and saw for myself.

Four decades on from those years, though, it's a different achievement that I want to commemorate: the part Keith and Paulette played in their grandchildren's lives. Before the 1960s were through, three (of four, eventually) arrived in quick succession, all born into failing marriages, which didn't take long to fail entirely, and when they did, Paulette and Keith became – certainly for my two children – their emotional anchor, the point of constancy in their unstable world of shifts and reversals.

On the death in 1974 of their step-grandmother Agnès, Paulette and Lili inherited two substantial properties in Auvergne: the Tourdes family business in Aurillac – workshops, stores and equipment, a three-storey house – and the country retreat at Jallès, twenty-five kilometres to the west. Paulette saw Jallès as her opportunity to set up a family seat of sorts, and bring her scattered family together for summer holidays. First, she and Lili agreed that the business in Aurillac must be sold. Thanks to their position and potential, the premises were valuable, but they needed to be restored or redeveloped. The business had ceased functioning years before. Floors had rotted, windows were smashed, machinery rusty. Agnès's living quarters had become a health hazard. For the thirty-five years she survived Albert, she'd lived like a squatter in three rooms. When Paulette braved them, she found cats nesting among collapsed furniture, objects strewn about, the kitchen sink piled high with unwashed dishes and cutlery. In the bedroom, she found a wardrobe and a clothes cupboards packed with unwashed pots and a few saucepans of congealed food crawling with insect life. For the best part of a week, and protected by a face-mask and rubber gloves, she cleared and cleaned and scrubbed. But the day she found a rat staring at her, she threw in the towel and called in the cleansing department.

The Jallès property was a different proposition. Though without much charm, it was solidly built and in good shape. Its situation was splendid too, with sweeping views across the meadows to some high Puys. It was a ten-minute walk from the station that was served by fast trains to and from Paris. With five ample bedrooms and plenty of extra floor space, Paulette saw that all the family could be there together at a pinch. She talked about it with Lili, expecting a thumbs-down as Lili had always said she'd never set foot in Auvergne again. On the contrary, though, she was enthusiastic. And so, for the next ten years, groups of us, small or large, would descend on Jallès for weeks at a time in high summer.

For the first two or three of them, we followed a routine. Before lunch, work on the house; sawing, hammering, nailing, painting, scrubbing, polishing, fetching and carrying. Paulette would marshal us, allocate tasks. Mine was to crawl into the roof space to brush tins of an anti-woodworm liquid called Xylophene into the floor and the beams. I'd come down at lunchtime stiff-kneed and reeking of chemicals. After lunch, we'd pile into our cars and drive to the *plage aménagée*, the artificial beach at the head of the St-Etienne-Cantelès dam. We'd bathe, chat, laugh, snooze. In the evening we'd put a couple of tables together in the garden, spread a cloth, drink the *gentiane* aperitif that was not everyone's favourite, then settle to a meal that went on until the stars appeared and we had to fetch pullovers.

Those memories belong almost entirely to our first summers in Jallès, because, as the years went by, Paulette and especially Lili lost heart. It was more demanding to look after the house and garden than anticipated. Problems mounted – the roof lost tiles in storms; the septic tank kept overflowing; and dry-rot was suspected despite my efforts with Xylophene – and though Lili was better placed to deal with them, it was Paulette who ended up doing so from England.

There was a second issue. It was more tricky to get to Jallès than we'd kidded ourselves. Despite the excellent trains, the most convenient way to travel with small children was by car. But that was quite an expedition. Once we'd got down to the Channel and crossed it – by ferry, as the tunnel hadn't yet been built – it was late afternoon and we were faced with a long slog through France in our small, slow cars. We'd break the journey somewhere and pitch the tents we'd borrowed. The next day we pushed on, but even when we had only a hundred and fifty kilometres left, the worst of it was still awaiting us, the grind up the switchback road onto the high plateau of Auvergne. We had to do it in stages, breaking the climb several times to let our Renault 4s and the children cool down.

But it was a third issue that made Paulette, Keith and Lili decide that the house should be sold. Their age. By the early 1980s all of them were into their sixties. Retirement was approaching. They'd want to reorganise their lives, and besides, physically they were slowing down. So the house was put on the market, where it lingered for over a year, and eventually was sold for a song.

Keith retired in 1983, two years after Paulette, two years later than normal as he'd needed to plug the hole in his pension caused by his period away from the profession. St Catherine's School had been delighted to hang on to him, and would have let him go on teaching indefinitely.

They'd remain in England, but the problem was where. For Paulette, it was Crawley; for Keith, anywhere but. Twenty years of it had made him determined to leave. He wanted to be in Dorset. But Paulette refused. She was equally determined. The house was what mattered, and hers in Crawley was the most comfortable she'd known in this country.

At the height of the standoff, Keith phoned me. He came straight to the point. Could I meet him the next day? Yes, but at what time? I'd be lecturing most of the day. Do you have an hour at midday? Yes. Right. He'd arrive on a late-morning train, buy me lunch and return to Crawley in the afternoon. And that's what happened. I met Keith at the station. He looked ill. The eczema on his hands was raw. He looked preoccupied. He'd come, he said, to prepare me for something big. He was going to be living in my area, at least for a while. He'd paid a month's rent in advance on a bedsit in Torquay. He was *that* close to walking out on his wife of forty years. He'd chosen Torquay, he said, because it was the West Country, and he could see more of my two children. As he didn't wish to inflict himself on us, Torquay was about the right distance. I asked him if he'd told Paulette his plan. Not yet, he said. He was still hoping she'd change her mind about leaving Crawley. Moral blackmail, I thought but didn't say.

He did tell Paulette, and she didn't budge. Keith duly came to Torquay. I went to see him in his bedsit. He had a bed, an armchair, a table, a wash-basin, an electric fire, a small fridge, a toaster and a Baby Belling. He seemed genuinely content. It was just right, he said. He'd get himself his breakfast, spend the morning reading, go down towards the harbour for lunch, walk around, take a bus somewhere perhaps, and in the evening he'd heat himself a tin of his favourite tomato soup. He'd join the town library. He'd book himself on coach trips; he'd seen an advert for an excursion to Newquay, another place with happy childhood memories.

My father stayed in that forlorn Torquay room for two months, waiting for Paulette to relent. When she did, he returned to Crawley, and the next I knew was that the two of them were doing a tour of the West Country to see if they could agree on somewhere to live. They couldn't. Paulette was as hostile to the west as Keith was to Crawley. It looked like deadlock again. I don't know if Keith had run out of fight, but he then offered a compromise. He'd accept East or West Sussex, Kent, Hampshire. They looked around the places they knew, Chichester, Midhurst, Arundel, Haywards Heath. But even the most modest house in those towns was beyond their means.

It was their old pacifist friend from Hounslow College days, John Barker, and his wife Judy who proposed a way through. They'd retired to Battle. They'd been investigating the housing market in East Sussex. There was good-quality affordable property if Keith and Paulette would consider somewhere on the coast, such as Hastings. But there was one agreement that Keith and Paulette had reached easily: not a seaside town, especially not in Sussex, especially not Hastings. But maybe because it was their one area of agreement, that's exactly where two months later they bought a house. Not exactly Hastings, to be fair, but as good as. They were moving to St Leonards-on-Sea, which is joined at the hip to Hastings, the way Hove is to Brighton. Their house, no. 8 Wingate Close, was in a horseshoe of semis in the high part of the town and, principally to please Paulette, out of sight and sound of the sea. It was a neat and well-built house, a box titivated with mock-Regency bay windows and a balcony too small to use. There were tall trees all around, suggesting the close had been built in a clearing of a wood.

Paulette and Keith had done their homework. They were near a bus route; the hospital wasn't too far; there were some local shops and a big Sainsbury's a short drive away. Keith had checked that there were clubs and activities to keep him occupied. First, he joined John Barker as a guide for the National Trust in Battle. Then he did the training to become a voluntary advisor at the Citizens' Advice Bureau. He went a few times to watch Sussex play cricket in Hastings or Eastbourne. He joined a bowls club. But centre-stage in their social life, Paulette's as much as Keith's, was the Hastings Anglo-French Club. Within months of joining, they were asked to run it. Keith was only too happy. Every year he put together its programme. He found guest speakers from all over, university professors, retired diplomats, anyone who had something worthwhile to say about France. He gave presentations himself. He picked my brains,

I remember, about *Le Grand Meaulnes*, the classic French novel of childhood I too had been researching. I looked at it as a story that had happened only in the participants' dreams, but Keith was less fanciful and more interested in the physical presence of, the Sologne country, drawn to it by its beauty and because it was so close to Auvergne. Paulette was active too; she gave two evenings on the folklore of Auvergne, one of them a practical demonstration of how to dance the *bourrée*.

The days in the Jallès house may have been over, but Keith and Paulette didn't stop going to France. In the summer, they got into their car and drove down to stay with Rolande and Jean-Christophe Benoit in their refurbished farmhouse a hundred kilometres south of Paris. Usually Lili was there, other friends too, and that beautifully-appointed house in its acres became the regular gathering-point for generations of Tourdes and Sorrells as Jallès had been. Most guests were happy to spend the day shopping, cooking, swimming in the pool, tending the garden, gossiping. No so for Keith. He needed projects. He'd spread maps and look for something of interest in these wheat-lands of the Beauce to take back to the Anglo-French club. He'd plot a route and set off in his car. He went to Sens and learnt about the cathedral; he found out all about the exquisite Briare aqueduct and the canal it carried; he visited the Abbey of Saint-Germain d'Auxerre. He'd return in time for supper, usually outdoors, followed by conversation (no television) and Scrabble, which everyone played but only Jean-Christophe and Keith cared about winning.

Chéroy was the ideal staging-post on the route to Auvergne, which is where Keith and Paulette always headed for. They'd base themselves in Aurillac, at the Hôtel de Bordeaux. From there, they'd tour the sites of Paulette's childhood, and beyond, to Saint-Flour, Mauriac, Riom, Maurs, Vic-sur-Cère. It was a golden age for them. Keith found a deeper pleasure in Auvergne than he had in earlier years, and I think Paulette did too.

Then, suddenly, in the first week of 1994, Keith died. Paulette broke the news incrementally. I arrived home from the university to find Claire waiting with a message. She'd taken a call from Paulette. I was to phone her the moment I got in.

"Ah, *titi*. How are you?"

"I'm very well, *mère*, thanks. And you?"

"Yes, yes, thank you. But your father ..."

"Not so well?"

"No. He was taken ill earlier today."

"Oh. Nothing bad, I hope."

"Well yes, it was rather sudden. He was at his bowls club finishing his lunch."

"I remember, he plays on Wednesdays."

"This time he couldn't, I'm afraid. An ambulance had to be called."

"Oh Lord."

"He fell to the ground. Apparently he was already unconscious."

"What are you trying to tell me, *mère*?"

"I'm afraid it was too late."

Claire was ready with a tumbler of brandy. Paulette was still on the line, saying that if I didn't mind, she'd better ring off. She wanted to tell Micou next, then Neil, in the correct order.

At his bowls club, having lunch prior to his match, Keith had announced that he wasn't feeling well and was going to go home. The team would have to call up a reserve player. He'd stood up, then fallen like a stone. He was dead before he hit the floor. That, we'd learn, is how it went with aortic aneurisms. When they burst, thankfully the victim knew nothing about it. It was that quick, and there was no pain.

Except for those left behind. It's pointless to weigh the impact of sudden death against death foreseen, but that's precisely what we started to do. Keith's departure without so much as a goodbye had caught us out badly. How selfish! But anger when gave way to grief, Micou had the worst of it. She'd seen Keith much more recently than Neil or I. I'd last seen him alive the previous summer on Paddington station after a family gathering in Kensal Green Cemetery to rededicate the grave of his grandfather Walter Peart, the heroic engine-driver who'd died saving his train. Neil hadn't seen him for well over a year. But Micou had, only a fortnight before he died. She'd spent Christmas with him and Paulette in St Leonards, and had given him a hard time for not appreciating the work Paulette had put in to make it a festive few days. Now Micou was berating herself.

The funeral packed out the chapel at Hastings Cemetery. We'd no idea so many people had known Keith. We were so grateful they'd turned out for him. There was a reception at his bowls club. After, I went for a walk on the beach.

The following day, we all left, and for the next weeks Paulette shut herself away and howled.

She re-emerged calm, accommodating and positive, as though she'd put the loss of Keith behind her. In one way, that was hard to accept; in another it was a relief. She was going to survive, and survive well. I remember thinking that this was the real Paulette, Paulette the peasant-girl from a land where no one could afford to linger over death.

We asked Paulette if she'd think of going back to live in France.

"Why?" She asked, "what would be the point?"

"The point? It's your country, isn't it? Your language, your culture? Anyway, the weather's better and so is the food. And you wouldn't have to hear any more tiresome jokes about the French."

"No, I'm used to England and it's too late to change. The one who *should* have lived in France was your father."

She had a point. Keith would have been the happier of the two in the country of Descartes, of logic and abstraction. There's a version of an old joke that's built on a key difference between French and Anglo-Saxon attitudes. An English engineer demonstrates to a French colleague an ingenious piece of machinery he's invented, and by trial and error has got to function. Impressive, says the Frenchman, but will it work in theory? Keith was the Frenchman in that joke. He needed systems and rules, and it was one set of rules, the highway code, that he was following the afternoon he almost crashed our car with all of us inside. A car was closing in on us from a minor road. It was obvious that its driver wasn't thinking about any rules. Paulette warned Keith that it wasn't going to slow down. But it must, Keith said, it's in the highway code. There's no must about it, Paulette yelled, use your eyes. Keith yielded, and let the other car pass. It didn't make him angry. It wasn't that he'd come off second-best. Simply, he was puzzled. Why would anyone ignore the rules? Because that's how people are, said Paulette, sounding like the English engineer.

One year after Keith's death, Paulette sold up in St Leonards and went to live with Micou – in the West Country, of all ironies, where Keith had wanted them to move fifteen years before.

14

A Day Trip to Garches

Five years later, in the summer of 2000, Claire and I were on holiday in Crete. We'd rented a small flat for a fortnight. We returned one evening to find a note under the door: ring Micou ASAP. I did. She told me there'd been a horrific accident that morning. Rolande, Lili and her friend Colette were being driven from Chéroy by Jean-Christophe to have lunch in a restaurant somewhere near Sens. On an almost empty road, an oncoming car had lost control, veered across the carriageway and smashed into them. Rolande had sustained a broken arm and leg; Jean-Christophe had critical head injuries and had been placed in an induced coma; Colette had a few scratches on an arm; but Lili had been killed outright. I stood back for a moment, then asked if Paulette was able to speak. She was. She sounded calm. She insisted we mustn't cut short our holiday, there was no point. Once we were back, yes, she'd need our help. As Lili's only surviving relative, the funeral arrangements and then all the bother with solicitors would fall to her. Two weeks later, we were steeling ourselves for Lili's burial in the village where the accident had happened and where she didn't belong. And a month after, Neil was driving Paulette and me to Paris in his Ford estate to empty Lili's flat. It was two days of problems. The worst, the heavy furniture, we solved by giving it to the nearest hotel on the condition they collected it themselves. A lot of things went into bin-bags for the Emmaus charity, and sentimental items were loaded into Neil's car for redistribution in England.

Now, in June 2008, I'm taking the early morning flight to Paris to have lunch with Rolande and Jean-Christophe. In the years since the accident, they've both been back to hospital several times: Rolande to have bones re-set, Jean-Christophe for surgery on his brain. They've had to sell their country property and move into an apartment in Garches, on the western fringe of Paris. I'm bringing Jean-Christophe the bottle of Drambuie he's asked for, though I'm surprised he's allowed alcohol, given what he's been through.

We take off and head out over the Channel. Half an hour later the captain comes on to tell us that soon we'll be able to spot the D-Day beaches of Normandy – Utah, Omaha, Gold, Juno, Sword. I must remember to tell Jean-Christophe. The Second World War has become one of his obsessions.

Rolande and I agreed last night on the phone to rendez-vous somewhere we both know very well, Place du Marché in Neuilly, where we used to go with Mitoune to do the shopping.

I get to Neuilly well ahead of the appointed time, as I want to look for Mitoune's *pension*. But, try as I might, I can't find it. The number I'm looking for, 21, has vanished, and the façades and shop-fronts are unrecognisable. I give up, go to a cafe on Place du Marché. I sit watching the bustle of market day. I finish my coffee and cross to the market, which has started to wind down. Stall-holders are yelling their final bargains – *soyez aimables, mesdames*, take these endives, cauliflowers, cherries off my hands. Half price, less if you give me a lovely smile. I buy a large *chèvre fermier*, knocked down to three Euros.

At twelve on the dot, I hear a car toot its horn and see an arm emerge from the passenger window and start waving. It's Jean-Christophe. I jump in the back seat and Rolande straightaway is edging us out into the traffic. At the same time she reaches her free hand towards me. I squeeze it, say *bonjour* and land a kiss on it. I look for Jean-Christophe's hand. But he can't turn. He can hardly rotate his head or his upper body, as though constrained by a brace. So I pat his shoulder instead. Rolande is driving as fast as she always has, seeing everything, missing nothing. She and I swap titbits, saving the real stuff for later. Jean-Christophe takes no part. He's looking for something, and near Suresne, finds it. This is where they were executed, he says, then goes silent again. What he's referring to, Rolande explains, is that imposing house on the hill. It's there that Resistance people were tortured and shot. I'd like to know more. I try Jean-Christophe but get no answer. There's no point, Rolande signals in the rear-view mirror, he's back in his own world.

We arrive in Garches, turn into their street, rue des Quatre Vents, Street of the Four Winds, and drive down the slope to the underground garage. It's when Jean-Christophe insists on getting out of the car unaided that I realise what that awful accident has done to him. Up until then – he was aged seventy-five – he'd been nimble and quick-witted. Now, his movements are mechanical. There's something of the automaton about him. I see too what the accident has done to Rolande. As the lift is out of commission, we have no choice but to use the stairs to their apartment, all eighty-eight steps. We know the number because Jean-Christophe counts them, four flights of twenty-two. Rolande doesn't say anything, but she seems in pain. She's still agile, but every so often she pulls up and holds on to the banister, grimacing. The fact is she has metal pins in her right leg and her left arm. I try, again, to relieve her of the bags she's carrying, and this time she lets me take them. Does she believe humping bags is women's work? Maybe; she's of that generation. More likely, though, she's refusing to be defeated.

We go into the apartment. Rolande knows what Jean-Christophe will do. He'll go straight to his study. To do Sudoku. He does several a day. He loves figures, patterns, quizzes. But anything involving emotion, he can't do anymore, nor imagination, nor fantasy.

"*C'est bien, bien triste,*" says Rolande, all very sad, "*mais c'est comme ça,*" that's how it is. She proposes a glass of champagne. Jean-Christophe is called. He's changed into slippers and a yachting blazer. I ask if he still cares about his appearance. Yes, but not so much, says Rolande. We drink a toast, *L'Avenir*, the Future. Not happiness, good fortune or wealth, simply the Future. Rolande proposes a second toast. To Lili, the friend she mourns every single day.

"*A notre pauvre Lili. Chin-chin!*"

Rolande and I sit back and go on chatting. Jean-Christophe, who isn't interested because one of his quiz shows is starting, positions himself in front of the television. He answers most questions: "Mussolini – a Chinese delicacy – Tiblisi – a bone in the foot – 1815". Every lunchtime it's the same, say Rolande. We leave him to it and go out onto the balcony. The view stretches over pavilions and lawns and tennis courts. At the horizon is the Forêt de Saint-Cloud. We might be a thousand kilometres from the high-rise slums of the notorious *banlieue* of Paris. Garches is an expensive and sheltered cocoon. I imagine that down there it's a world of bridge parties, men in tartan caps walking Pekinese dogs in body-warmers, readers of the tabloid *Le Parisien*, and supporters of Le Pen.

It's time for lunch. Rolande disappears into the kitchen. She hasn't drunk much of her champagne. She tells me to stay put and finish it for her. In apartments all around, the curtain has risen on the daily theatre which is the French Lunch. Rich meaty aromas are reaching me. Then Rolande calls me indoors. Jean-Christophe is at the table, knife and fork already in his hands, napkin under his chin. He's impatient and lets us know it.

We eat *saucisson* and grated carrots in a vinaigrette, then *escalopes* served sizzling from the pan. Rolande and I eat slowly, chatting, but Jean-Christophe races ahead and in no time, he's pushing away his empty plate and calling for his *crème caramel*.

Her mouth still full, Rolande gets up and fetches it. She sees my expression, sighs and says: *il faut se faire*, got to get on with it, what choice is there. Lunch has become disjointed, no longer the choreography you expect in France. Jean-Christophe consumes his *crème caramel* and clears a patch of table to set up a game of cards: Patience. Rolande brings in strawberries for her and me. We pick at them while Jean-Christophe moves cards around, fast and dextrous, until he's got the right result. Now it's time for his coffee. Rolande goes back to the kitchen to prepare us all a cup. Jean-Christophe remembers the Drambuie I've brought. I tell Rolande I'm surprised that he's allowed alcohol. He's not, she says, but it's not really a problem because after one sip he loses interest.

When the quiz show is over, Jean-Christophe switches off the television and goes to sit on the chair by the front door. He's making it clear that he wants us all to go out, like a dog asking for its walk. I raise an eyebrow. Oh, says Rolande, he does that every time someone visits. She hurries to get herself ready, but her leg is giving her gyp. I say that she should simply take me to Saint-Cloud railway station, three streets away. She won't hear of it. Nor, she whispers, would Jean-Christophe. The plan has been made, and he can't abide any changes.

Twenty minutes later, we're on the Pont de Suresne, crossing the Seine. Unlike this morning, Rolande's route takes us through the Bois de Boulogne. Jean-Christophe alerts us to a grotto with a waterfall and weeping willows, a kitsch Marie-Antoinette kind of Arcadia. Those willows, says Jean-Christophe, are paddling their feet in water. I'm taken aback. It's the only time he's said anything involving his imagination. Have I heard right? Is there a part of his brain that still can do metaphors and similes?

His attention is soon drawn back to the traffic, which has become very heavy. He tells Rolande how she must deal with it. This is what you do, this not that; where you overtake, here not there; when you signal, now not in five seconds. All day long, Rolande has been the model of restraint and good humour, but now she cracks. If this *bonhomme* of hers doesn't like the way she drives, she'll stop the car and he can get out and walk. His response takes me aback, again. He breaks out into one of his smiles of old, and becomes the charmer he was before the accident. He turns the few degrees he can towards Rolande. What would I do without you, *Bibi*, he asks. Rolande, eyes front as we swing out onto avenue de la Grande Armée, answers that he'd be fine, absolutely fine, as he's always been. He'd find a way, he'd turn that smile on some poor sap, female of course, and she'd rescue him. You always fall on your feet, she says, *toujours, toujours, toujours*. You're the great survivor. So good luck to you, and now be good enough to let me drive.

We reach Porte Maillot, where I'm to get the airport shuttle bus. Because the traffic gives no quarter, there's time only to put on the hazard lights and pull in to the kerb. I reach over the seats and grasp first Jean-Christophe's hand, then Rolande's, and thank them for a marvellous day, a wonderful lunch. We must do it again, says Rolande. *On ne rajeunit pas*, we're not getting any younger. I lean further over and manage to plant a kiss on her cheek, near her ear. I think of doing the same to Jean-Christophe, but he's not playing ball. He's looking for gaps in the traffic. I get out, and as the car pulls away, I wave. Rolande flutters a hand. There's nothing from Jean-Christophe. He's looking straight ahead.

The next day, when I phone from Exeter, they must be out doing their morning shop. I listen to Jean-Christophe's recorded message. *Je voudrais savoir si j'ai été appelé.* I should like to know if I've been called. A curious form of words, and imperious. The voice is as it's always been, so well trained that even a phone message sounds like opera. The voice is the one part of him that the accident hasn't touched. But it's a cruel illusion. At the other end of the line, he's no longer there.

15

A Week in Wells

Wells, July 2008; my morning coffee hour, my last before I'd be returning to Exeter. I was in the Swan Hotel across from the cathedral. At the next table, three Gurteen-clad gentlemen, all wearing club ties, were discussing the readings for a special service that sounded very High Church.

I was taking a break from my duties as Paulette's Designated Carer. That had been my title for the week. I'd borrowed it from Micou, who'd gone at last to spend some time with her husband in Geneva. She hadn't been away properly since 2004, the *annus horribilis* when Paulette fell, broke the same leg twice in three months, and lingered half the year in hospital.

She'd come home to Wells that autumn in a wheelchair. Home was Micou's house in St John's Street, where they'd lived for a few years. Paulette had a bedroom and her own little study-cum-sitting room. The arrangement and Wells itself suited her better than Micou's previous cottage in Brent Knoll, to which Paulette had moved a year after Keith's death. Micou was teaching just a few miles away at the Quaker school in Winscombe, so it was mainly for Paulette's sake they'd moved further off to Wells. There was nothing for her in Brent Knoll, a dormitory village without shops, library or community centre. She'd got through the days with only Micou's cats and parrot for company. Wells, by contrast, had all she wanted: shops, a library, concerts, a cinema, the University of the Third Age, new friends.

So she'd been delighted finally to be back from hospital. Over time, she'd regained a degree of mobility, and had kept as active as she could. Now, though, four years on and aged ninety-two, she'd slowed down. She knew what that meant; this was, she said, her *final lap*.

I was in The Swan partly to be out of the way of the carer Somerset Social Services sent every morning to wash and dress Paulette. I'd said hello to today's, Helen, who'd arrived a few minutes after eleven, running late. Paulette would make her even later. It was demanding work to get her up and functioning. I'd discovered five days before just how demanding. She'd twisted herself into an impossible position, and I'd needed some force to untangle her. I'd had to handle intimate flesh, which we'd both been too embarrassed to mention.

I stayed on in the Swan until I felt sure that Paulette was ready, washed and combed, dressed smartly to keep up her morale: skirt, silk blouse, embroidered jacket, and a brooch and rings. I knew I'd find her installed among the books, records and CDs that Micou's had assembled for her. She might have put on a record so that in her chair she could dance a seated *bourrée*, one foot forward, back, side, other side; then the other.

My week in charge had begun nervously. Over the months I'd been finding it more and more difficult to adjust to Paulette's rhythms, stay patient about them. On the drive up from Exeter, I wasn't at all sure how I'd find my mother. I needn't have worried.

"Hello, *titi*, hello," offering up her cheek for my kiss.

"How are you, *mère*?"

(How did I expect her to be? Silly question.)

"*Tout va très, très bien!*" Everything was absolutely fine.

As it had gone six o'clock, I set about supper, a pan of ratatouille Micou had left for me to re-heat. After, Paulette had wanted only half an apple. And then her nightly battle to stay awake had begun. She'd started a conversation but fallen asleep mid-sentence. We'd tried a few more times, then turned to the television, but that hadn't helped. Give in, *mère*, I'd said. Go to bed. No, not yet. We'd resumed our conversation but it had fizzled out. At nine-thirty, Paulette finally had capitulated. On her zimmer-frame, she'd got to the foot of the stairs, trans-ferred herself and her bag of tricks, – pills, ointments, lotions, tissues, wipes – onto the stair-lift, and ascended. Above my head, I'd heard the step-step-clump, step-step-clump along the landing. Then silence until her bedside radio had come on. I'd allowed another fifteen minutes before going up with her glass of water for the night. I'd made a lot of noise to give her warning, positioned myself at her door, and called out for per-mission to enter. A long pause, then "Yes, *titi*, come in." But too late to stop me seeing more than I wanted. In parking her-self on the edge of her bed, she'd opened her nightdress and I'd been shocked to see just how black and purple, mottled and blotchy, her skin had become. I'd retreated and waited on the landing. When I'd been called in again, Paulette was half sitting, half lying, in a tangle of sheets and pillows. I'd watched her slowly sort it out. Finally she'd lain back, closed her eyes, and admitted she was *flagada*, whacked. But then, a minute later, her eyes had re-opened and she'd given me a smile that seemed to come from a different person, the bright little girl she must have been. Feeling I was twice her age, I'd smiled back, put her glass down on her bedside table, checked that her phone was properly in its cradle, and lowered the vol-ume on the radio, knowing that she'd turn it on in the night. I slept in the room next to hers, and didn't want to be woken. I'd kissed her goodnight. She'd reached up an arm, touched my face and given me another of those smiles.

The next morning, a little before seven, I'd tiptoed out onto the landing and gone downstairs. I had an hour to myself before Paulette's *levée*. I knew this would take about twenty minutes, and then I'd hear the whirr of the stair-lift's motor. Paulette would transfer to her zimmer-frame, and reach her armchair. And so it had been. She'd drunk the tea I fetched her, swallowed her pills and tablets ... And then she'd started to talk. And talk, for an hour without interruption. Her subject had been the old battles, with Mitoune, Pitou, Keith and ultimately with herself. It wasn't one of the rages I remembered from childhood. It was more controlled than in the past, but no less exhausting.

I'd stopped her by getting up and suggesting breakfast. Paulette had got the message instantly and asked me to forget the *radotages*, the ramblings of an old woman. And it was she then who'd suggested I should take myself off to the Swan Hotel. I went every morning, drank a pot of coffee and wrote a journal of our week, along those lines:

On Tuesday 15th July, we had a late lunch, and as Paulette was reasonably alert and the weather fine, I suggested a breath of air. We both needed it. She accepted, and was happy to go wherever I chose. I got her arms through her jacket and prepared the wheelchair. Setting her feet in the footrests and fastening the safety-belt took a bit of doing. I'd not planned an itinerary. Let's just see where we got. We started in Silver Street and reached the recreation ground where Paulette made me stop so she could enjoy the breeze catching the trees. From the bowling-green came the knock of wood on wood. We skirted the bandstand, and a hundred yards beyond, the moat around the Bishop's Palace. We moved into the precincts of the cathedral and past the west face, and eventually came out on the old Shepton Mallet road. We took a path that wound down to a cricket field. A petrol-mower was striping the grass alternately light and dark. Paulette took much pleasure in the groundsman's skill. She called him an artist. Then we were at a rugby pitch, overgrown and out of season. Paulette worried that I was getting tired. Not at all, I said, and meant it. Pushing her along was no great effort. I didn't add that it was because she'd lost so much weight. I said we were like St Cuthman and his mother. Paulette had forgotten the legend so I told her of the eighth-century boy who wheeled his mother in a barrow as far as Steyning, and to honour his pledge to God, began to build a church with his bare hands. When he couldn't lift the huge cross-beam to start on the roof, a hooded figure Cuthman took to be Christ appeared, floated the beam into place, and vanished – the miracle to which Cuthman owed his sainthood.

We'd been out two hours and Paulette was tiring. We set off for home. We passed the cathedral once more, its west front fiery in the sun. Ten minutes later, we turned into St John's Street and entered the house. Even on a bright afternoon such as this, the ceiling-beams kept it dark.

At four the next morning, I couldn't sleep so I got up and stood on the landing outside Paulette's room to check. Silence. The silence went on. Could it be normal, no sound at all? Should I go in? Then there was a snort and the rustle of bed clothes. Still alive.

Two afternoons later we were sitting in front of the television. Paulette was trying to keep up a commentary on the programme, but was falling asleep mid-way through a sentence. Not unusual of course, but this time her head rolled and flopped about, and her breathing became raucous. There was a watery rumble in her chest I'd not heard before. Premonitions, I wondered.

I suggested we go out and wake ourselves up. Good idea, she said. On foot, without the wheelchair. She wanted to see how far she could walk. We started out along the flat, easy pavement, towards Southover. She had one of her sticks and she had my arm. But it was so slow, much more than last time I was here. We stopped every minute for a rest. After fifty yards, she said we must turn back, and leaning on her stick, stared me in the face, saying nothing. I returned her gaze, waiting for her to say something. But she went on staring. I wondered if she was having a stroke. Then she spoke:

"Oh *titi*, I'm such a parasite. How do you put up with me?"

At four on my final afternoon, I took a cup of tea to Paulette in her study. She was sorting through old letters, notes, papers.

"*Ah, ça tombe bien*," she said. Good timing; she had a couple of things for me to take home. The first resembled a long, thin matchbox whose lid read "J. & J. Cash Ltd, Coventry". Inside were a few woven name-tapes left over from my days at Steyning Grammar School. There was nothing I could do with them, yet I didn't want Paulette to throw them away. The second item was a letter with my name on the envelope, written in Paulette's hand.

"I've copied this out four times, one for you, Micou and Neil, the fourth one for my GP. Take it please, but don't read it now."

Which, five minutes later alone in another room, is what I did. It was what I'd suspected: Paulette's living will. If and when her physical condition became irreversible, it read, she wanted there to be *no* attempt (underlined twice) at resuscitation, *no* effort (underlined twice) to prolong her life. But she wanted every bit of pain relief she could get.

I returned to her study and told her that I'd disobeyed her and read the letter. She said she thought I might. But, I went on, what if we couldn't bear to follow her wishes if and when the time came?

"Then you'll have to be very brave. I mean every word of what I've written."

It shouldn't have, but that letter read like a death warrant Paulette had written and signed herself.

Two hours later, I was ready to leave for Exeter as soon as the carer showed up. My bag was packed, the car outside. The doorbell rang and Helen, whom we'd not seen since the first day of my week, was there. I would leave them to it. From her chair, Paulette reached up an arm to me. The gesture was saying, let's do this sensibly. Let's not waste words, certainly not on what will be happening in a month's time. Yes, by September, she'd have left Micou's house for good. At her own insistence she was moving into a Home. She'd be better off there, she insisted. But the real reason, Micou was sure, was to relieve her of the burden of care. And it wasn't making her, Micou, the slightest bit happy.

16

The Lap of the Dogs

Weston-super-Mare Hospital on a bright day is not unattractive. The rounded contours and soft brickwork, the trees and landscaping, suggest a science park or a university. But when you've been tailing a loved one's ambulance in the dark, as Micou and I had, you're not interested and can't see much anyway. All we cared about, that Good Friday of 2010, was that Paulette should be settled in a bed and seen by a doctor, quickly.

"Some hopes," said our paramedic. "A Friday night?"

He led the way. Our destination turned out to be not a ward but a corridor. There, Paulette took her place in the queue of trolleys. Our paramedic left to get himself signed off and onto the next job. It was a little after ten pm. The wait, we found out from the nurse we managed to buttonhole, would be long; there was only one doctor on duty in A&E. Was she serious, we asked. Afraid so, she replied. We pretended to Paulette that we'd soon have her out of the place and back home. She smiled up at us.

"It's in the lap of the dogs."

Twelve hours earlier, at home in Exeter, a couple of old friends down from Oxford had come to lunch. Midway through, the phone had rung. Micou. Could I come up as soon as possible? Paulette had taken a sudden turn for the worse. It looked like pneumonia. The Home had called the doctor. He was due sometime in the afternoon. I'd apologised to our guests, packed an overnight bag, and ninety minutes later I'd arrived in Axbridge.

It was Paulette's second full-time Home in a little over two years, though since 2005 she'd been going occasionally into Fletcher House in Wells to give Micou some respite. Those short visits had worked out well, and had given Paulette confidence ahead of the permanent move in 2008 to a Residential Home in Draycott, not so permanent as it turned out. After some months, she'd begun to need round-the-clock care, and that meant the Nursing Home in Axbridge.

Here, as in Draycott, Micou had done everything to make Paulette's room remind her of St John's Street – her recliner had been brought in, her desk, framed photographs, pictures to hang on the walls, a pile of books, a radio, a music centre, CDs and a cupboardful of clothes.

On the way upstairs to Paulette's room, I passed Micou who was talking to a nurse and looking at some paperwork. I left them to it and went up to Paulette. She was in bed and seemed very pale. She made an effort to greet me, but sank back onto her pillows. She was sorry for the bother she was causing. I tried to get her to drink something, tea, water. With no luck. When Micou came in I made three cups of tea, but again Paulette refused. We sat by the bed, we talked a bit, we waited. It was almost nine o'clock by the time the doctor arrived. He apologised for the lateness, but he'd been run off his feet. You wouldn't believe, he said, how many people chose to fall ill on a public holiday. We left the room while he examined Paulette. It didn't take long. It was indeed pneumonia.

An hour later, Paulette's trolley was lowered from the ambulance and we followed it into the hospital. It was 1 am before she reached the head of the queue and was wheeled into a cubicle. The doctor arrived. She was about thirty, professional, polite, harassed and utterly exhausted. She went round

Paulette's chest and back with her stethoscope, tapped this rib and that with her fingers, asked some questions, and re-confirmed pneumonia. Paulette would be admitted onto a reception ward. We asked the doctor if it was true she was the only one on duty. Yes, it was true. Shouldn't we say something? I wish you would, she replied. They'd listen to you.

The twenty days it took Paulette to die went in four stages, each in a different place. One: reception ward. Two: long-term ward. Three: side-ward. Four: individual room. Most of those twenty days, Micou visited, then phoned Neil and me to report: good days and bad nights, or bad days and better nights. For almost two weeks, we didn't have a sense of which way things were going. Neil and I were downbeat; Micou stayed hopeful.

On her good days, Paulette was delightful company. On middling days, she could still joke and make reasonably light of things. But on bad days, it was awful. To cover her mounting distress she'd go on the attack. One evening Micou phoned me in floods of tears. All afternoon, Paulette had savaged everyone in sight, but particularly Micou. Nobody was listening to her, Paulette was shouting. It was dreadful. Micou thought that if she'd been able, Paulette would have struck her a blow. I tried to say it was the pain talking. Well of course it's the bloody pain, said Micou. And it was she who was having to soak it up. It was never Paulette's lovely boys who got it in the neck. Our dear mother would have miraculously pulled herself together if we'd shown up. I do know, I said. The trouble was that our mother came from a society that still didn't value daughters as highly as sons. And how exactly does that help, Martin? It was a fair question.

Paulette's thinking was modern, in most ways, but not about gender politics. Like many women of her generation, she had little time for it. It was the indulgence of young women who didn't know they were born, demanding rights that weren't rights at all. They should be concentrating on their children.

But, I felt, the more Paulette argued her case, the more it sounded like guilt. Guilt that she had gone out to work herself when the three of us were still small.

From time to time, when Micou and I were visiting Paulette together, we'd slip out to Palm Springs, the hospital's cafe and discuss the future. Micou was growing confident that Paulette would be discharged before very much longer. Micou wouldn't let her go back to Axbridge or anywhere else. But she might have to, I said. What about Fletcher House again? To my mind, that was the nicest, and of course it was conveniently in Wells. I'd not found it depressing to visit Paulette there. We'd walk up and down a corridor to get Paulette more mobile, with good results. Or we'd sit in the lounge chatting and gossiping about the residents. They were a varied bunch. There was one, Harry Patch, who'd become famous as the last soldier alive anywhere in the world to have fought in the First World War. Why didn't Paulette tell him about Pitou at Verdun? No, said Paulette, Harry liked talking to television interviewers, but not to anyone in the Home. He spent the day seated on a sofa, his medals pinned to his blazer, holding the hand of a lady resident and conducting his love affair in silence. At the time Paulette was in Fletcher House, he was one hundred and seven years old. When he died, in 2009, he'd reached a hundred and eleven.

So, Micou said, definitely no more Homes. Paulette was coming back to live with her in her new house in the Somerset countryside. And there she would look after Paulette until she died, whenever that might be. A downstairs room would be adapted for her. The views from her window would recall Auvergne. Paulette wouldn't be short of company as Micou would soon be available all day now that she was about to retire from her school. Meanwhile, there'd be the television and the radio, as many books as she could read, records and CDs too. And since her eyes were still good, she could sew and darn. There'd be the cats to keep her entertained, and when Micou got home, she'd wheel Paulette out to look at her hens and ducks and geese or take her for a walk.

It was an ambitious plan, and a generous one. But there was one snag: no human company. Paulette was gregarious and sociable, and the nearer she was to death the more she needed the buzz of life around her. Just how much was brought home to me during another spell she'd had in hospital a few months earlier. We'd taken her away for an hour to see a Home near Weston which we thought she'd like, a handsome mansion in its own grounds. But as we left the road and houses and approached it down a dark, wooded lane, Paulette was grew agitated. And when we walked into what must once have been the ballroom where a solitary resident sat immobile, Paulette started to tremble.

"No, no, take me away. Now."

We drove straight back to the hospital, where Paulette installed herself in her favourite chair in *Piccadilly Circus*, as she called her ward.

A few days after the pained phone call from Micou, I walked in on Paulette and saw immediately that any plan to bring her home was doomed. Something in her demeanour had changed. She was done for, and she knew it.

"Don't look at me like that, *titi*. I'm not afraid, you know. But don't forget my instructions in that letter. I'm serious."

It was then that she asked to see all the family. She'd long since done the practical work of departure: wills, insurance policies, heirlooms and possessions distributed. What she wanted now were private audiences. That meant Micou's husband Alex; Neil, Susan and their son Dominic; Neil's daughter Ingrid, her husband and their children; my daughter Anna, her husband and their two girls. It should have meant my son Marc, his wife and their two children, but as they now lived on the other side of the world, Paulette thought it was too much to ask.

By the time of the audiences, she'd had been moved to her third ward, smaller, quieter, with some beds unoccupied – odd, given the crowding everywhere else in the hospital. I assumed it was the anteroom to the morgue. It was there that over a period of days, one by one, the family filed through. Micou didn't need an audience, of course, and as I visited pretty regularly, neither did I.

After the audiences, Paulette picked up and had a few good days. She and I shared jokes and anecdotes. The one we liked best was about the seventeenth-century grammarian Claude Favre de Vaugelas, who, on his deathbed, is said to have declared: "*Je m'en vais ou je m'en vas. L'un ou l'autre se dit ou se disent.*" The closest I can get in English would be: "I will or shall soon die. One and/or the other is or are grammatically correct." Vaugelas must have been a humourless pedant, we decided. Or maybe a self-ironist.

And there was the ritual at the end of every visit:

"*Allez oust!* Off you go. See you either here (a gesture towards the chair) or (a finger to the sky) up there."

Paulette was transferred next to a small room of her own, adjacent to her first ward and near the matron's desk. This I supposed was from anteroom to death-cell. I was about to enter it one afternoon when a nurse stopped me. I should be warned, my mother was a bit delirious, talking a lot but making no sense. I went in and heard:

"*Aiga – soif – tengo sed – aiga – necesito agua – j'ai soif.*"

It made perfect sense. The words, a mixture of French, Auvergnat patois, and Spanish, were about water. She was parched with thirst.

Things continued to go badly. Two days later, Claire and I found her half propped up, half bent, and yelling a monosyllable over and over.

"Seet!"

I obeyed and fetched a couple of chairs. Claire tried to get Paulette to lie back properly, and was rebuffed. So we sat down, but all that did was to make Paulette more frantic.

"Seet!"

We tried to tell her that was exactly what we'd done.

"Seet!"

"*Mère*, what do you *mean*?"

"*SEET!*"

We were completely at a loss. All we could do was to stay seated and try to act normally. Did she need anything, a glass of water, a cup of tea, food?

"*SEET!*"

The force she put into that sound, I thought she might break a bone. I was close to tears. Claire suggested I go off and have a cup of tea downstairs. I did. By the time I returned, Paulette was asleep. The nurse had given her a sedative. She said that it wasn't at all uncommon for pneumonia patients to have these psychotic episodes.

But on the drive home, it dawned on me: *seet* was aimed at Paulette herself, not us. She'd needed to be in a sitting position; the one she'd got herself into was causing her excruciating pain, for which she'd been given nothing stronger than paracetamol for fear of depressing her breathing. There'd been nothing psychotic about it.

It went from bad to worse. The weekend of 17th and 18th April was awful. Micou phoned me late on the Sunday to report the four visits she'd made in the space of forty-eight hours. The hospital had been even busier than usual. The wards were full to capacity but there were fewer nurses on duty and she'd not been able to find a doctor at all. So Micou had done everything herself. She'd snatched coffee and biscuits when she could, and had cat-napped in an armchair. She'd been home only to feed her animals. Now she was drained. She asked when I was coming next. Tuesday, I said. Not tomorrow, Monday?

No, I had an unbreakable commitment. Well, that's a pity, said Micou.

By 10:30 on the Tuesday morning, I was at Paulette's bedside, knocked backwards by the distress she was in, the worst I'd seen. Her eyes were shut, and I wasn't sure whether she'd heard me come in. One of her feet was exposed, and I was shocked to see how misshapen it had become. It looked like some kind of root. Her breathing was uneven; gasps, rattles, then silence. I went in search of a nurse, who had to quieten me down. The consultant was on his rounds and would be here very shortly. Would I like her to bring me some tea? I said yes. A few minutes later the consultant entered, accompanied by a registrar and a student. He was handed Paulette's notes, which he studied and then passed to his colleagues. A discussion followed. Paulette opened her eyes and tried to speak, but not enough air was passing over her vocal chords. All that could be heard was a rattle which contained a few vowels and consonants. I leant right into her face, and she tried again:

"*J'ai mal – fini.*" It hurts – finish.

I straightened up, turned, and shouted:

"For god's sake, this woman is dying. Give her some bloody morphine!"

I dropped into a chair and started to shake. I heard more discussion, then the doctor and his team left. The nurse put a hand on my shoulder and told me that morphine was on its way.

The next evening, Wednesday, Micou phoned. I braced myself for the worst, but her voice was bright. She'd spent most of the day with Paulette, who'd been on the best form since she'd arrived in hospital. I couldn't believe it. After I'd put the phone down, I realised I felt not only relieved but baffled, deceived even. Someone was playing a macabre game, and I didn't know if it was the Grim Reaper or Paulette.

An hour later, my daughter Anna phoned. She had the next day off from work, so what if she and I went to see Paulette together? If we got to the hospital by ten, we could spend a couple of hours with Paulette and be back in time for Anna to collect her girls from school.

We arrived in Weston-super-Mare in bright sunshine. This hospital, with its grass and trees, really wasn't a bad place for Paulette to be. Anna agreed. We parked and entered the building. We waved to the nurses and pushed open Paulette's door. The room was dark. I'd expected to find the curtains open, the sun streaming in, and Paulette sitting up ready for us. But she was lying perfectly still beneath her bedding. Her eyes were closed. In forty-eight hours, her face had imploded, caved in on itself, and her head seemed the size of a pygmy skull. She'd turned yellow, the yellow of parchment. We stood rooted, not breathing. I asked Anna to stay put while I went to fetch someone. The matron was at her desk. Could she come, immediately please? She did. I asked:

"This is it, isn't it?"

"I'm afraid it is," she replied.

I needed to phone Micou, who was spending the day tending her animals. I tried to sound casual. Things didn't seem quite so bright this morning, I said. I heard the catch in Micou's throat. I suggested she have a coffee, then come over to the hospital. No real rush, but sooner rather than later. And drive sensibly. I returned to Paulette's room. Anna was sitting by the bed stroking the hand that lay on the covers. I drew up a chair on the other side and leant in close. Paulette's face looked like a carving on a tomb. She heaved a deep breath, and then she went so still I thought it was all over. But there was a second heave. Recalling that the last of our senses to go is the hearing, I brought my lips to Paulette's ear. I was amazed to see how extraordinarily long the lobe had grown, like some tribe's body deformation. I murmured: "Let go, *mère*." There was almost nothing from her now. No snorts, no rattle, just every so often a feather of air. Anna had turned her head away, and was continuing to stroke the hand on the blanket. I looked at my watch; it was 11:30. I needed to know the exact moment it happened. I went on speaking into Paulette's ear; stopped to check for breath; spoke again; stopped; listened. I repeated the cycle ten, fifteen times, before the truth began to spread through me that there was no longer someone in there for me talk to. There was no point in checking the time. Paulette had stopped while I wasn't looking, as imperceptibly as the hands on a clock.

I sat motionless; Anna wept quietly. Minutes passed. Finally I stood up, so did Anna, and on our way out to find the matron, she gave my shoulders a little rub. The matron accompanied us back into the room, confirmed that Paulette was dead, and extended her sympathy. She suggested Anna and I have a cup of strong sweet tea. She'd not do anything until Micou had arrived. In the Palm Springs cafe, I drained a mug of very sweet tea. Anna chose hot chocolate. We agreed we should head Micou off. Anna would stand sentinel outside Paulette's room; I'd guard the main entrance.

While I waited, I got on my mobile to Neil in York. I told him the news. He didn't say a word. After a few seconds, I asked if he was still there. He was. What would happen now? Well, Micou was on her way, and the hospital protocol had kicked in. Neil asked if it had been a peaceful death. I said I hoped so.

Micou arrived. As we walked towards Paulette's room, I broke the news. Her reaction was not what I'd anticipated. She got busy. First she tidied Paulette's hair, then smoothed the bedclothes. She cleared the mess on the bedside table and started to gather Paulette's belongings. Anna and I needed more hot drinks. Why didn't Micou join us in the cafe when she was ready? She agreed. Twenty minutes later she was with us. Anna fetched her a chair. I got her a mug of tea.

"So."

"So."

"Orphans now."

*

167

Ten o'clock on the morning of 10th May 2010. The early clouds had dispersed and the weather looked promising. Claire and I had arrived at a car-park in Cheddar not far below the Gorge to rendezvous with the other principals – Micou, Neil and their cohorts. A silver-haired couple was already waiting for us. We shook hands.

"I don't believe we've met before."

"If we have, it's too recent to remember."

Not counting this couple, there'd be thirteen of us to distribute among the three vehicles which would follow Paulette's hearse. The burial ground was over twenty miles away, if you drew a straight line, which Micou hadn't. She'd plotted a route to take Paulette through the Gorge and over the Mendips, which had always reminded her of Auvergne.

The hearse arrived, quiet as a ghost. I swallowed hard. This time she really *was* leaving. She'd nearly done so once or twice before, but to her frustration her body had held out. Four men emerged. In the spring weather, their full-length coats looked wrong. One, who couldn't have been more than nineteen, too young for this trade, drifted out of sight, at a guess for a smoke. I walked over and looked through the windows at the flowers arranged around the coffin, which was made of wicker and could have served as a linen basket. My eyes smarted. It had been two weeks and a half since Paulette's death, and I thought I'd be readier than I was.

The long coats reconvened. It was time to get the convoy under way. Anna, her husband and their two girls took their places, followed by Claire and me, in the limo directly behind the hearse. Both vehicles, I noticed with some pleasure, were not black but a satisfying pearl grey. Micou and Alex had chosen to follow in her car; Neil, Susan and Dominic in theirs. The silver-haired couple brought up the rear. We started out towards the Gorge and ran straight into a road-block. Several police-cars straddled the road, their blue lights revolving. An officer was working her way down the line of traffic to tell us that there'd been "an incident". That was all the explanation we were getting. Some vehicles were doing three-point turns to make their escape. I got out to see what more I could discover. The rumour going round was that a car had smashed into a boulder at high speed, deliberately. The road would be closed for most of the day.

There was only one thing for it: we turned as well and headed to the M5, which as ever was fast, crowded and aggressive. We edged in one by one and gathered speed, then ran into our second obstacle. A caravan had overturned and spewed its guts across all three lanes.

"The number of times that happens," said our chauffeur. "Those things should be banned."

It took us nearly half an hour to filter through on the hard shoulder. As elegantly as we could, we powered ahead. We reached the Avonmouth Bridge. Down below, the wasteland was still packed with brand-new cars and vans, row upon row of them. They never seemed to shift, I said. There had to be a good few hundred. Oh, a hell of a lot more, said the chauffeur, all going abroad while our idiot government let us import thousands of foreign ones. Didn't make sense. Well, you know, market forces, I said, then changed the subject. Would we get to Woodlands on time? The chauffeur saw no problem.

Twenty minutes later we left the motorway. Anna's two girls, who'd dozed off, sat up. We followed the hearse through one set of lights, then a second. At the third, the hearse decided very suddenly to put on its indicator and swerve right. Our limo did the same. I looked round to check that Neil, Micou and the silver-hairs had seen. They had. All turned right. The road we were on began to get very rough. This looked wrong. Instead of open country, we were on a building-site of half-finished houses. The road was soon a mud track. The convoy halted. An angry conference took place. Hadn't these undertakers heard of satnav? We'd have to double back. From here on in, Micou would lead the way.

She spun her car around and moved to the front. The hearse turned, then our limo went for it, forward on full lock with so much accelerator pedal that the front wheels smacked into a kerbstone the driver hadn't seen. The impact was violent. We got out to inspect. The bottom of the right wing had been forced up against the tyre. The chauffeur tugged at the metal, and managed to pull it clear enough to allow us to continue. The tyre wasn't damaged, so he said. No need to change the wheel. We had to take his word for it. We manoeuvred and rejoined the convoy. Micou led us back to the correct route. The syncopated squeals of our flapping wing and possibly a damaged bearing turned heads as we went, fast as we dared, racing against the clock.

With three minutes to spare, we made it to the Woodlands burial ground. Our priest, standing at the chapel door, sprang into action. He went inside, gave the nod to the man on the sound system, and the first piece of music Neil had chosen began to play. By the time the long-coats had the coffin on the move, we'd composed ourselves and taken our places in the front two pews. And to the accompaniment of flutes and recorders, we rose to our feet as Paulette made it to her last appointment bang on time.

17

The Hour Always Strikes Twice

From the windows of our little plane I see why Auvergne has been called an island surrounded by land. Claire and I are coming to Aurillac to spend a few days looking at where Paulette's story began. It's my first visit in almost forty years and Claire has never been. As we step into a taxi at the airport, I tell her to listen for the Midi accent, the nasalised vowels, the heavily rolled "r". But our young driver, though born and bred in Aurillac, she tells us, doesn't have the slightest trace. It's not of her generation. We need to go higher up into the remote villages where there are many more old people, or further down into the Cévennes.

She deposits us at the Hôtel de Bordeaux. Someone is playing the Flight of the Bumblebee on the piano in the lounge. I open the door. A tiny girl perches on the stool, head bent over the keyboard, hands flying. She can't be more than ten. Her mother sits close by, sewing. When she's finished, she drops down from her stool and gives us a grave bow. The mother tells us that they're Japanese, naturalised French. They live a few streets away, and whenever she can she brings her daughter here so that she can use Aurillac's finest piano.

It's coming up to 11 am and we need coffee. We like the look of the Café Mary. It stands at one corner of Square Vermenouze, Aurillac's focal point. We park ourselves on the *terrasse* to get the best of the sun. On the far side of the square is the church of Notre-Dame-aux-Neiges, Our Lady of the Snows, a poetic sort of name for the great hunk of basalt it is. On the upper side of the Square, the Palais de Justice, the law court, is imposing at the top of its flight of steps. Further down there are shops, a hotel, a bistro, and the awning over the entrance to an underground car-park. At the table next to us sit a stylish couple, Parisian at a guess. The woman looks as brittle as a twig in her black dress. The man wears a suede jacket and matching moleskin trousers. His scarf is an architecture of powder-blue. On the pavement opposite there's a group of people with dogs. An elderly woman in a baseball cap and white shoes is hurrying past, carrying her chihuahua. Another woman is emerging from the Carrefour store with full shopping-bags on both arms. Ahead, beyond avenue Gambetta and the River Jordanne, is Puy Courny, the hill that encloses Aurillac on its southern side. Courny's varied green tones remind me a little of the Sussex Downs.

The church clock starts to strike eleven. The chimes are full and round, and carry on the air. When they're done, I start to tell Claire about my last visit to Aurillac. The square was less luxuriant then, fewer trees and hedges, and I don't recall the water feature that's there now. It was emptier, I thought, but even so I wondered where the crowds of people found the space to dance their *bourrées*. I'm saying this when Our Lady of the Snows starts her eleven chimes again, and I remember. Of course, of course, that's what happens in this part of the world. Paulette always said that if you heard a clock strike the hour twice, you knew you were south of the Loire.

We leave the coins for our coffee on the table – this isn't Paris; customers are trusted – and drift towards rue des Carmes. The business premises of Paulette's grandfather Albert were somewhere round here, on rue J.-B. Rames. The photo I have with me, taken in 1974, the year Paulette and Lili inherited the property, shows a set of buildings in a sorry state, so dilapidated in fact that it seems they were pulled down very soon after. A block of flats now occupies the site. I take a few photos, then we head for the old quarter. We pass a photography shop, where a rack of old postcards on the pavement outside catches my eye. They're all studies of Auvergne and portraits of Auvergnats. I choose a dozen, including one of a *cabrette* player in traditional dress. On the reverse is the first line of the *bourrée* Paulette once tried to teach us, *L'aïo de rotso té foro mourir, filhoto!* The water from the spring will kill you, girl! It's the start of a morality tale about the poisoned waters of adultery as opposed to the limpid stream that is marriage.

We reach rue du Rieu, the street of Mitoune's ill-fated shop. The sun scarcely finds a way in, it's so dark and narrow. For a weekday morning in the centre of a departmental chief town, it's eerily quiet. But our taxi driver did say that Aurillac has been haemorrhaging inhabitants, around a thousand a year, she thought. Claire checks on her phone. In 2000, the population was 36,000 and has steadily declined, though now it's levelling out. As many people are moving in or being born as are leaving or dying.

I'm trying to work out with Claire which of the tall thin properties was the Tourdes shop when somebody – he could be one of the blow-ins – comes over to us.

"English people in Aurillac!" he says.

He couldn't help overhearing us and wonders if we need any help. Mostly, I think, he wonders what on earth has brought us to this town. We explain. He's an interesting and obviously highly-educated man. He looks urban and prosperous, but not flashy. He has excellent, idiomatic English. It's our turn to be intrigued. He tells us he runs an international business consultancy. He was based in Paris, but he and his wife wanted a healthier environment for themselves and their kids, somewhere rural but with an airport to connect him to the rest of the world. Aurillac ticked all the boxes, he says. Right size, clean air, mountains, lakes, good schools. And, he freely admits, no racial tension. He tries to help us locate the shop. It could be either one of two, we decide. The houses have probably been renumbered.

In the evening, we return to the old quarter, looking for somewhere to eat. But there's nowhere, not even a cafe or a bar. The town is dead. We go back to Square Vermenouze where we have seen one restaurant. We go in, sit, study the menu and decide on the *formule*, the set-price meal that includes Salers beef and *truffade*. It sounds good, but it turns out to be a bad choice. We're served meat the size and consistency of a brick, and a *truffade* that's all potato and no cheese to speak of. Neither of us gets far. We call it a day and ask for the bill. Our waitress can't believe it.

"In Auvergne we work hard and eat properly."

Neil arrives in Aurillac the next day. Micou would have liked to come as well, but she can't leave her animals. As Neil will be here for barely twenty-four hours, the only plan we've made is to visit the Tourdes plot in the cemetery. We've never been sure which of the family lie there. Mitoune certainly isn't one of them, but Micou thinks Pitou is.

It's a long climb and the late-September sun is surprisingly strong. Nevertheless, we walk it, as Neil and I did one summer, 1970 or 1971, when Albert's ninety-year-old widow Agnès (she of the verminous saucepans in wardrobes) outpaced us all the way to the top. We catch our breath, then go across to the office of the *gardien*. He needs a good few moments to locate the Tourdes *concession* on his wall-chart. As he thinks we might not find it, he decides to accompany us himself.

Five minutes later, we're there. The tomb is a disappointment, a flat and featureless expanse of stone, and what's more it's been fractured by subsidence. At its centre there's a headstone inscribed *Albert Tourdes, 1871–1938*. Nothing more. The dates are hard to make out. A lot of the inscription is covered in lichen, which I try in vain to dislodge with my credit card. There's no mention of Agnès, and nothing about Pitou – Pierre, as it would have read. The *gardien* can't enlighten us. It's possible there *are* other Tourdes lying here as the grave was dug for four but there's no paperwork to tell him. He points out, as if we didn't see, that repairs are badly needed. But the authorities won't carry them out as the *concession* has expired. Whoever's buried under there will have to be transferred to the communal area. Though of course we're welcome to pay for the repairs ourselves. None of us, I fancy, will be doing that.

The next day, Neil goes back to Toulouse to pick up his flight back to England. We see him off on his train. As Claire and I leave the station, we pass a rough sleeper – the only one we've come across in Aurillac, I realise, just as we haven't seen more than two, maybe three faces which weren't white. He's got up to relieve himself against a wall. Claire says something innocuous to me, but he hears an insult:

"*Je pisse où je veux, mes amis.*"

The world is his pissoir.

"*Nous sommes en FRANCE, pas chez Madame Thatch-AIR!*"

The lady's name waved with his free hand.

We decide we'll carry on and have a walk up Puy Courny, Paulette's favourite bit of Aurillac, perhaps because it recalled Jussac. We cross the Jordanne and follow avenue Aristide Briand away from the town. Already the beeches and chestnuts are shedding their leaves; the pavement is yellow and slippery. At Chemin du Barra, we turn left and the climb stiffens. We pass the last chalet house and we're in the open, higher than we'd imagined. Already the town is a distance below. In the field to our right a herd of cows is on the move. They're Salers, which Paulette talked a lot about in her last years. She thought them the finest of breeds, intelligent, alert, nimble as goats. And – she liked to add in a spirit of mischief – the opposite of lowland cattle, so fat they keep flopping down and so lazy they can't be bothered to get up.

I can't judge the Salers for their intelligence, but I can admire them for their looks, the wide curve of their horns, the russet pile of their coats. And as we start to make our way back to the town, their bells' melody follows us down the hill.

The next day is our last, and we've reserved it for a visit to Jussac. The sky again is blue and cloudless, the sun as strong as it was yesterday. We've come to find where Paulette was born and where it all began. It's my first time here as well as Claire's. The taxi has dropped us at the north end of the village. Somewhere round here is, or was, Grand'mère's house. We walk to the bridge over the river Authre. "River" seems a big word for the trickle below. I can't see how it could have rinsed a week's worth of Grand'mère's washing. But when we clamber down to the water's edge, it's deeper and faster flowing than I realised. The banks are thick with reeds and grass, and underfoot the ground squelches. It must have taken strong arms to push a laden wheelbarrow down and back up. At the top of the far bank stands a long grey building. A sign says it's a hotel, but it calls itself Le Pont de l'Authre; I don't see how it can have been the Chandon, Grand'mère's home, which Paulette said stood well back from the river. This building surely is too close. I must look elsewhere.

We set off towards the village centre, shielding ourselves as best we can from the articulated lorries, the majority with foreign number plates. Fifty metres along the road I spot a likely candidate, a solid grey house set well back. I can't tell. So I take a photo, hoping to match it up with something in our albums. We continue, but now to look for the church and the square which Paulette said was so busy that I thought we'd hear it well before we saw it.

Not a bit of it. There's nothing here. In fact I'm wondering if I've got the wrong place. I can't have, though, as the church is here and it's the only one in Jussac. It's a lot smaller than I'd expected. Its façade and outer walls are bright white and set with lumps of black rock. It puts me in mind of a Dalmatian dog, Claire of a plum pudding. But where's the square? Paulette's shops? The village square she described turns out to be a semi-circle barely deep enough for the fountain that spouts only geraniums. No cafe, no haberdashery? And then I see, yes, they *are* all here. There *is* a cafe. But it's closed, and the notice in the window suggests it's for good. There *is* a bakery too, but that's not functioning either. A sign says it's for sale. There are only two businesses still active. One is the butcher that does match Paulette's description. The other is a hairdresser's, which could have been the haberdashery she so loved. I think I'll ask. I take a peep through the bead curtain; there's a woman under a hair-dryer that wraps around her head like a brain-scanner. She's leafing through a magazine and hasn't heard me. Apart from her there's no one here.

It's time to move on. We have a plane to catch. I walk up rue de la Croix Longue, Street of the Long Cross, and find Claire. She's been pursuing an agenda of her own, searching for birds with her binoculars. She says she doesn't want to leave yet. In fact, not at all. She could live here. She's enchanted. She's understood why it made Paulette so happy. Couldn't we delay our taxi and continue up the hill, stay a few minutes more? I get on the phone and arrange it. Then we climb another kilometre and turn off into an orchard of cherry trees. We pass an empty farmyard. Five minutes later we're high enough not to see or hear traffic. There's scarcely any movement anywhere. The occasional bird, no insects. We still have time to absorb the view. To the west, against the sun, the naked eye can see almost as far as Ayrens. Eastwards, through Claire's binoculars, I make out what must be Marmanhac, where Mitoune and Grandmère and generations before came from, and set even further than Jussac into this remote corner of *la France profonde*.

177

And then it really is time to leave. We take a last look around, and set off down the hill to meet our taxi by the grey house near the Authre, and which in the end may be the one I've been looking for all along.